THE ROCK&GEM BOOK

...AND OTHER TREASURES OF THE NATURAL WORLD

WRITTEN BY **DAN GREEN**

DK India

Senior Editor Bharti Bedi
Project Art Editor Pooja Pipil
Editor Deeksha Saikia
Art Editors Tanvi Sahu, Vikas Chauhan,
Alpana Aditya, Sonali Rawat
Assistant Art Editor Priyanka Bansal
Senior DTP Designer Harish Aggarwal
DTP Designers Jaypal Chauhan, Nityanand Kumar
Picture Researcher Nishwan Rasool
Jacket Designer Surabhi Wadhwa
Managing Jackets Editor Saloni Singh
Pre-production Manager Balwant Singh
Production Manager Pankaj Sharma
Picture Research Manager Taiyaba Khatoon
Managing Editor Kingshuk Ghoshal
Managing Art Editor Govind Mittal

DK UK

Senior Editor Chris Hawkes
Senior Art Editor Rachael Grady
Jacket Editor Claire Gell
Jacket Designer Mark Cavanagh
Jacket Design Development Manager Sophia MTT
Producer, Pre-production Gillian Reid
Producer Vivienne Yong
Managing Art Editor Philip Letsu
Publisher Andrew Macintyre
Art Director Karen Self
Associate Publishing Director Liz Wheeler
Publishing Director Jonathan Metcalf

First published in Great Britain in 2016
by Dorling Kindersley Limited
80 Strand, London WC2R 0RL

CONTENTS

THE ROCK&GEM BOOK

...AND OTHER TREASURES OF THE NATURAL WORLD

Fossils 122

Shells 154

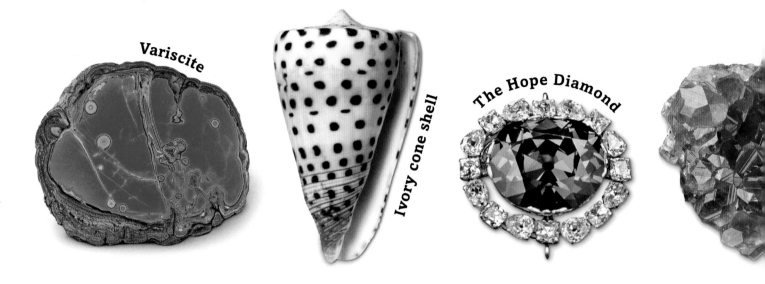

Variscite

Ivory cone shell

The Hope Diamond

Foreword

Our planet is bursting with wonders of nature. The rocks that make up Earth's surface hide countless surprises, from colourful minerals to glittering gemstones, and valuable metals. This book is a fascinating collection of natural treasures, along with the amazing fossils and beautiful shells.

Growing up by the sea in Wales, I was fascinated by the things that the tide brought in. With my sisters, I would scour the beach looking for treasures, collecting shiny stones, patterned pebbles, and shells. The hills around were dotted with lead mines, and I was obsessed with the idea of finding gold in local rivers. I never did find any gold, but sometimes I would turn up a rock with small fossil shells embedded in it, which was almost as exciting.

I went on to study geology at university. There I learned that, as well as being irresistable for their beauty and rarity, minerals tell us a story about how the planet formed and changes over time. Fossils record the tale of how life on Earth has coped with the challenges of living on our ever-changing planet. Rocks and minerals are important in our everyday lives, too. Many of the raw materials we depend on are dug out of the ground.

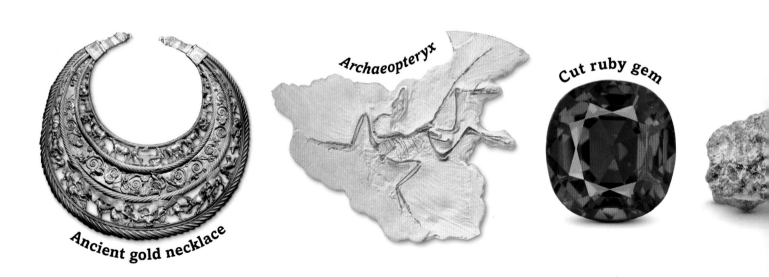

Ancient gold necklace

Archaeopteryx

Cut ruby gem

Moon rock

Hessonite

Azurite heart

Pine cone fossil

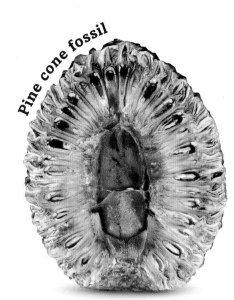

Inside this book you'll discover rocks and gemstones, encounter important mineral ores, come face to face with astounding fossil organisms, trace the history of life, and marvel at pretty shells. Along the way, you will see some of the most amazing landscapes and natural wonders. I hope it will inspire you with curiosity about the world around you and maybe even set you off on your own journey of discovery.

Dan Green

Throughout this book you will find scale boxes that show the sizes of examples of rocks, minerals, gems, fossils, and shells compared to either a child, school bus, or human hand.

Child = 1.45 m (4 ft 9 in) tall

School bus = 11 m (36 ft) wide

Hand = 16 cm (6 in) long

Lazurite in marble

Abalone shell

Bornite

Our rocky planet

Earth is a rocky ball, with thick, molten rock near its centre. Only a thin surface shell of the planet is fully solid. This crust is made of rocky minerals – mainly combinations of silicon and oxygen called silicates – and is up to 50 km (31 miles) thick. Earth is not a quiet place. Heat from inside the planet keeps the crust turning over. Large slabs of rock, called tectonic plates, are shunted about, causing earthquakes and fiery volcanic eruptions, and heaving up mountain ranges, as they bump and crash into each other.

How Earth formed

The planets of the Solar System formed at the same time, about 4.6 billion years ago, from the cloud of dusty rubble orbiting the Sun. Over millions of years, small clumps of this debris grew larger and were pulled into spheres by the force of their own gravity. As the sphere grew, it attracted more and more debris, accelerating the growth of our planet.

This artwork shows a sequence of how Earth formed – from small fragments of rock and dust sticking together to a planet that had its own atmosphere.

Ocean crust is between 5–10 km (3–6 miles) thick

Outer core is 2,300 km (1,430 miles) thick

Volcanic site above a "hot spot" in the mantle

Land surface made of continental crust

More than two-thirds of surface is covered with liquid water

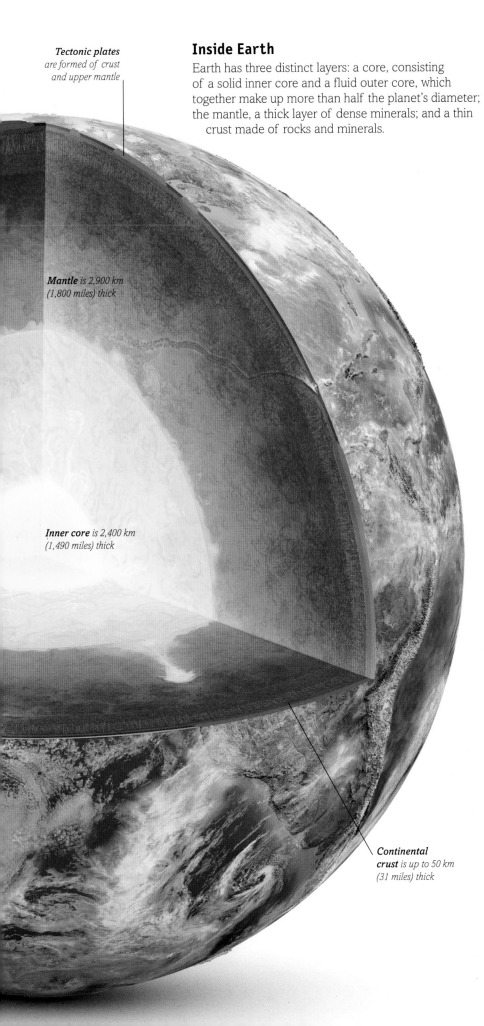

Tectonic plates *are formed of crust and upper mantle*

Inside Earth

Earth has three distinct layers: a core, consisting of a solid inner core and a fluid outer core, which together make up more than half the planet's diameter; the mantle, a thick layer of dense minerals; and a thin crust made of rocks and minerals.

Mantle *is 2,900 km (1,800 miles) thick*

Inner core *is 2,400 km (1,490 miles) thick*

Continental crust *is up to 50 km (31 miles) thick*

Moving plates

Earth's surface is divided into a jigsaw of interlocking slabs of crust and solid mantle. These huge blocks, called tectonic plates, move on the treacly mantle beneath the surface. There are eight major plates and many smaller ones.

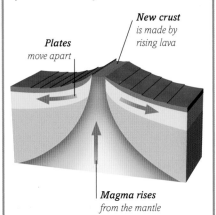

Plates *move apart*

New crust *is made by rising lava*

Magma rises *from the mantle*

Spreading

New crust is created where movement pushes plates apart. As the crust thins, magma rises to the surface and spreads lava over the surface. This happens along the Mid-Atlantic Ridge.

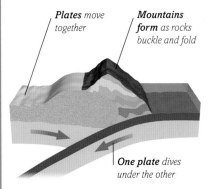

Plates *move together*

Mountains form *as rocks buckle and fold*

One plate *dives under the other*

Crunching

Crust is destroyed where plates come together. The higher plate rides up over the other as the lower plate dips down into the mantle. This pushes up mountain ranges, such as the Himalayas and the Andes.

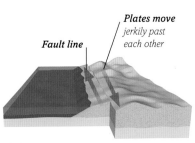

Fault line

Plates move *jerkily past each other*

Sliding

When plates move sideways, no crust is created or destroyed. The friction between the two plates builds up tension, which may release with a snap, causing earthquakes.

The rock cycle

Most of Earth's rocks are hidden beneath the surface, but in some places they are visible in the landscape: mountains, canyons, and coastlines, for example. Many different types of rock have developed over billions of years through a variety of processes. These include volcanic activity, which creates rocks at or near the surface (known as igneous rocks), the formation of sediments in places like the sea floor (sedimentary rocks), and changes in form brought about by extreme heat and pressure (metamorphic rocks). These processes are linked in a never-ending cycle known as the rock cycle.

Rock recycling

The planet endlessly recycles its rocks. Mineral grains worn off igneous rocks are deposited to form sedimentary rocks. Pressure and heat in Earth alters minerals to make metamorphic rocks. When rocks melt, a new generation of minerals crystallize out of the magma, creating new igneous rocks.

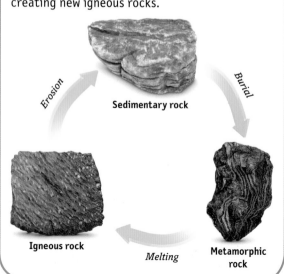

Erosion

Sedimentary rock

Burial

Igneous rock

Melting

Metamorphic rock

Water moving downhill under the influence of gravity carries mineral grains to the sea

Some sediments are deposited in sea beds

Sediments transported to the sea build up into layers on the edges of the continents

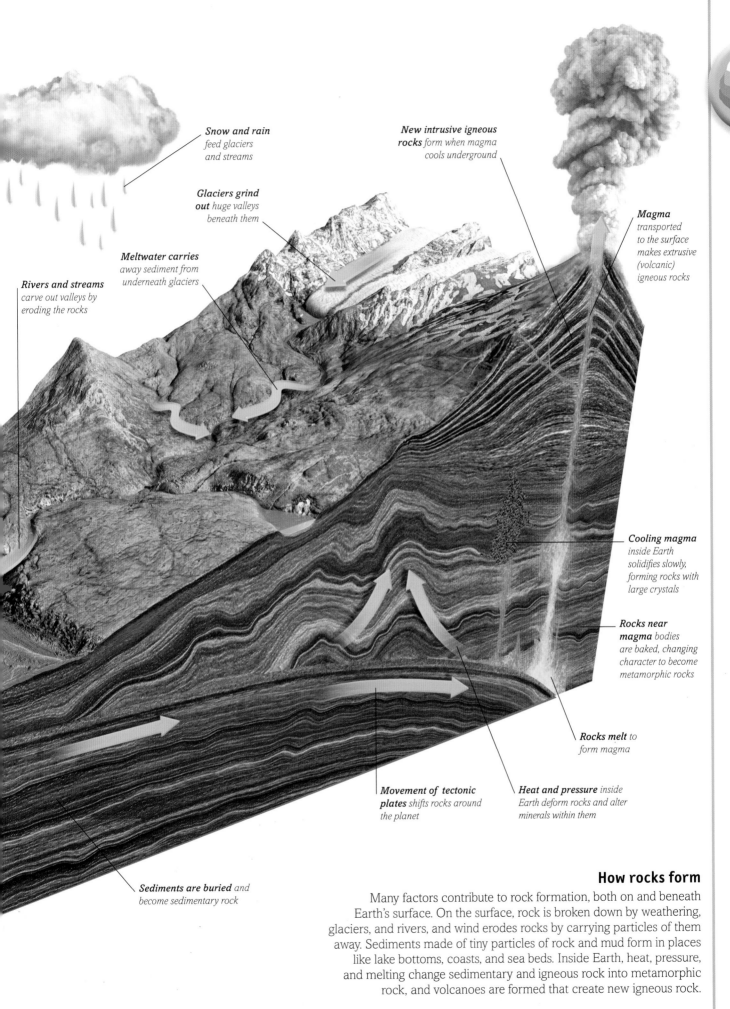

Snow and rain *feed glaciers and streams*

Glaciers grind out *huge valleys beneath them*

Meltwater carries *away sediment from underneath glaciers*

Rivers and streams *carve out valleys by eroding the rocks*

New intrusive igneous rocks *form when magma cools underground*

Magma *transported to the surface makes extrusive (volcanic) igneous rocks*

Cooling magma *inside Earth solidifies slowly, forming rocks with large crystals*

Rocks near magma *bodies are baked, changing character to become metamorphic rocks*

Rocks melt *to form magma*

Movement of tectonic plates *shifts rocks around the planet*

Heat and pressure *inside Earth deform rocks and alter minerals within them*

Sediments are buried *and become sedimentary rock*

How rocks form

Many factors contribute to rock formation, both on and beneath Earth's surface. On the surface, rock is broken down by weathering, glaciers, and rivers, and wind erodes rocks by carrying particles of them away. Sediments made of tiny particles of rock and mud form in places like lake bottoms, coasts, and sea beds. Inside Earth, heat, pressure, and melting change sedimentary and igneous rock into metamorphic rock, and volcanoes are formed that create new igneous rock.

11

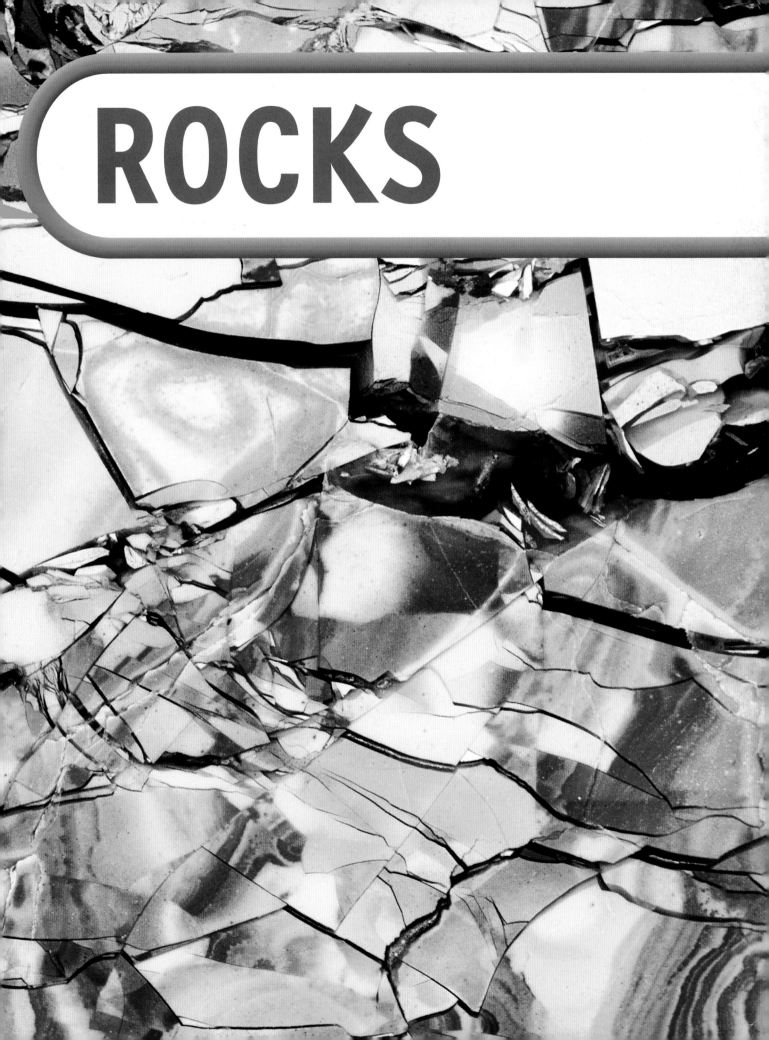

ROCKS

Rocks

Rocks

A rock is a naturally occurring material consisting of one or more minerals, although a few rocks are made of other substances, such as decayed vegetation (coal, for example). There are three major classes of rocks – igneous, sedimentary, and metamorphic – and each of these classes is further divided into groups and types, mainly based on their mineral composition and texture.

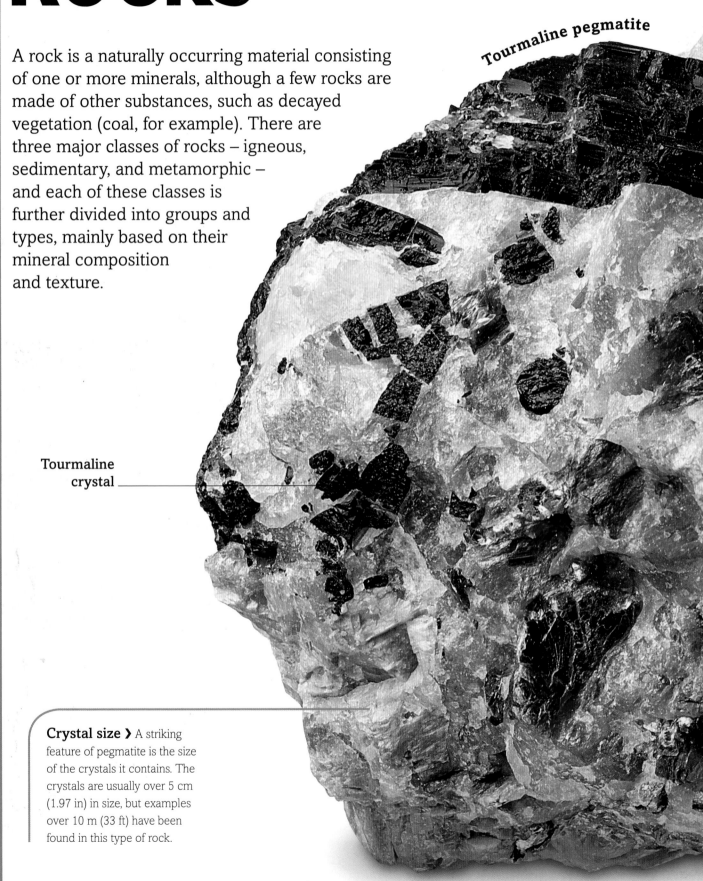

Tourmaline pegmatite

Tourmaline crystal

Crystal size ❯ A striking feature of pegmatite is the size of the crystals it contains. The crystals are usually over 5 cm (1.97 in) in size, but examples over 10 m (33 ft) have been found in this type of rock.

14

Formation ❯ Pegmatite is an extreme igneous rock that forms during the final stage of magma's crystallization. It is called extreme because it contains exceptionally large crystals, and because it often contains minerals that are rarely found in other type of rock.

Quartz

Types of rocks

Igneous
• Formed from molten rock (magma), which either solidifies underground or after it flows to the surface.

Sedimentary
• Generally formed from mineral grains deposited on Earth's surface by water, wind, or ice.

Metamorphic
• Formed from existing rocks that change when subjected to extreme temperatures and pressures underground.

ROCKS IN THE LANDSCAPE

Devil's Tower, Wyoming, USA. A rock that cooled within a volcanic vent and that has been exposed over time by erosion.

The Grand Canyon, Arizona, USA. The Colorado River has cut a 1.6-km-(1-mile-) deep canyon through layers of sedimentary rock.

Taigh Bhuirgh Beach, Harris, Scotland. Gneiss, a metamorphic rock, has distinct bands of minerals of different colours.

Igneous rocks

Granodiorite

Potassium feldspar gives a pinky colour

Kimberlite

Granite

Diamond embedded in rock

Salt and pepper look comes from white feldspar and black biotite mica

Peridotite

Pyroxenite

Coarse-grained dark rock

Green peridotite in volcanic rock

Dunite

Yellow-green rock is an important source of chromium ore

Deep inside Earth, it is hot enough to melt rock. At searing temperatures of 1,250°C (2,280°F), the red-hot, treacly, melted rock, called magma, forces its way up through the solid layers of Earth's crust along cracks and other lines of weakness.

Intrusive igneous rocks form when magma cools slowly beneath Earth's surface. Under immense pressure, the magma crystallizes and hardens into a rock. Made of interlocking crystals, they are tough and durable. Intrusive rocks have larger grains than volcanic rocks because they take

Gabbro

Porphyry

Coarse texture *of interlocking crystals*

Diorite

Fine-grained *rock contains large crystals*

Pegmatite

Intrusive rocks are called **plutonic**, after Pluto, the Roman god of the underworld.

Grains *are of similar size*

Green colour *results from mineral olivine*

Tungsten darts

Tungsten metal *on dart tips is extracted from pegmatite minerals*

Supersized crystal

Grey *feldspar crystals*

Anorthosite

Syenite

Light plagioclase *feldspar crystals*

longer to cool and the crystals have more time to grow. Coarse-grained **granite** is the most common intrusive rock. **Pegmatite**, a source of rare metals and gemstones, has the largest crystals of all. **Porphyry** forms when large, slowly growing crystals are cooled quickly and are surrounded by small crystal grains. Sometimes whole lumps of rock from Earth's upper mantle – the layer underneath the crust – form intrusive igneous rocks. These **pyroxenites**, **dunites**, and **peridotites** all contain lots of the mineral olivine, while some **kimberlite** rocks contain diamonds.

Granite

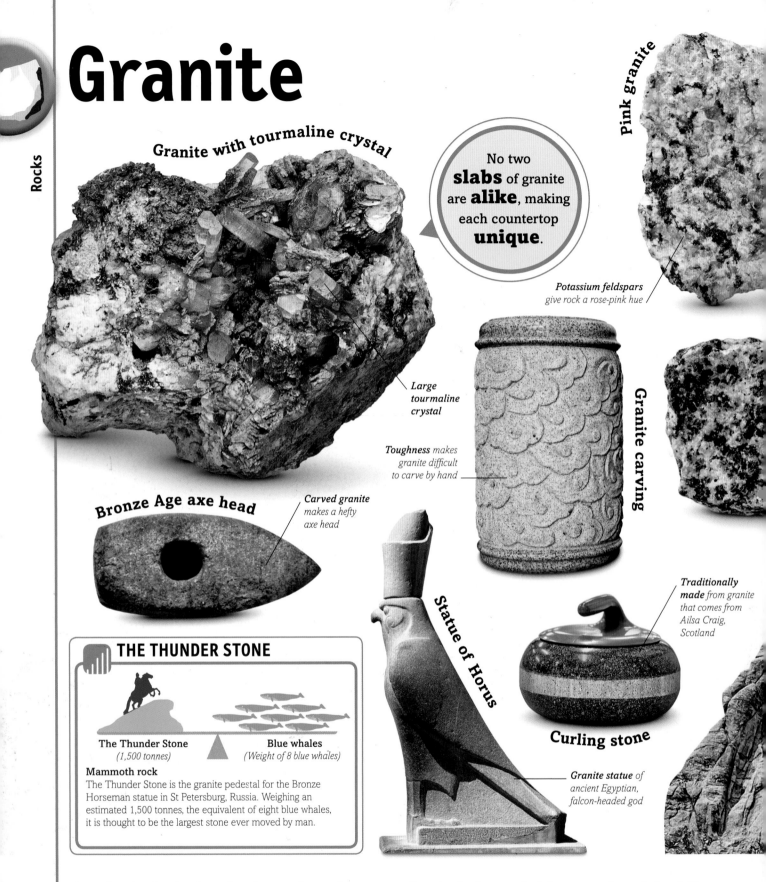

Granite with tourmaline crystal

No two **slabs** of granite are **alike**, making each countertop **unique**.

Pink granite

Potassium feldspars
give rock a rose-pink hue

Large
tourmaline
crystal

Granite carving

*Toughness makes
granite difficult
to carve by hand*

Bronze Age axe head

*Carved granite
makes a hefty
axe head*

*Traditionally
made from granite
that comes from
Ailsa Craig,
Scotland*

Statue of Horus

Curling stone

*Granite statue of
ancient Egyptian,
falcon-headed god*

THE THUNDER STONE

The Thunder Stone
(1,500 tonnes)

Blue whales
(Weight of 8 blue whales)

Mammoth rock
The Thunder Stone is the granite pedestal for the Bronze
Horseman statue in St Petersburg, Russia. Weighing an
estimated 1,500 tonnes, the equivalent of eight blue whales,
it is thought to be the largest stone ever moved by man.

Granite is the bedrock of our planet's crust. The foundations of the continents are underpinned almost entirely by this coarse-grained, intrusive igneous rock. Granite makes up no less than 70 per cent of Earth's crust.

Granite is the symbol for strength and durability. The most common intrusive rock on Earth, it crystallizes slowly from silica-rich magma deep underground. Magma is often injected into the crust in enormous quantities. These rock masses are called batholiths. They often remain as tall

Made from Cheesewring granite from Cornwall, England

Tower Bridge, England

Polished stones used for flooring and countertops

Granite slabs

Granite statue dates to around 1250 BCE

Bust of Ramesses II

Black specks of hornblende produce a mottled appearance

Hornblende granite

Porphyritic granite

Large crystal of plagioclase feldspar

Trégastel, France

Rocky granite peak called a tor

Mount Rushmore, USA

Carved out of the solid granite cliff face, each ex-president's head is 20 m (66 ft) tall

buttresses after the cover of country rock has eroded. **Trégastel, France**, and **Mount Rushmore, USA**, are examples. Granite is a mix of three main mineral crystals – feldspar, quartz, and mica. The type of feldspar and the mix of minor minerals give the rock its distinctive colours, of mottled white, grey, and even **pink**. When polished, granite's large crystals glitter from countertops and the façades of buildings. This unyielding rock has been used throughout history for making **stone tools**, **statues**, and **busts**. Rough-hewn **slabs** are used as cobblestones and cut as building blocks.

Volcanic rocks

Trachyte

Rough-textured lava
is light-coloured

Volcanic ash
has solidified

Lithic tuff

Hollow, air-filled pores make pumice so light it can **float on water**.

Texture has
many gas bubbles

Needlelike crystals
look like snowflakes

Snowflake obsidian

Glass rather than
mineral crystals

Volcanic, or extrusive igneous, rocks are born of fire. Magma hits the surface at temperatures of 1,200°C (2,190°F). Bubbling and fizzing with dissolved gas, it explodes violently through volcanoes or oozes slowly from a vent or fissure.

Volcanic rocks form when lava cools and solidifies. They have small grains, because they cool quickly giving crystals little time to grow. **Basalt**, **andesite**, and **trachyte** are the most common lavas on Earth. Because it is so thick, **rhyolite** magma can cause the most violent

Pele's hair

Mount Fuji, Japan

The core of Mount Fuji is composed of andesite

Andesite

Light-coloured crystal

Molten lava is spun out by the wind into long, hairlike strands

Basalt

Rhyolite

Pink banding is not common

Pumice

Rich in iron and magnesium

Bread crust volcanic bomb

Hard outer crust like a loaf of bread

Edge on arrowhead is sharper than steel

Arrowhead

Obsidian

VIOLENT VOLCANOES

Yellowstone, USA, 640,000 years ago
A massive eruption, it produced 2,500 times as much ash as Mount St Helens.

Mount Tambora, Indonesia, 1815
The largest eruption in recorded history, it caused a yearlong winter around the world.

Mount Pinatubo, Philippines, 1991
Second-biggest eruption of the 20th century. Many people were evacuated before the eruption.

Krakatoa, Indonesia, 1883
Made the loudest bang ever recorded. This massive eruption triggered tsunamis, killing many people.

Mount St Helens, USA, 1980
Deadliest eruption in American history. The explosion blew the top off the mountain.

eruptions. Most lavas are made up of silicate minerals including feldspars, olivine, amphiboles, micas, and quartz. **Tuff** is rock formed of volcanic ash, which is sometimes hot enough to weld together. **Obsidian**, a black volcanic glass, cools too quickly to form crystals. During volcanic eruptions, volcanoes may shoot out lumps of lava called "**bombs**". Dissolved gases pump **pumice** full of frothy bubbles! **Pele's hair** – named after the Hawaiian fire goddess – is made of long, wispy, mineral fibres that are drawn out in the air as liquid rock erupts.

Basalt

Lava lake

Basalt volcano, Hawaii

Carved from a single block of basalt, the stone weighs 24 tonnes

Sun stone

Ancient hand axe

Vesicular basalt

Holes left behind by gas bubbles during cooling

Lightweight, jagged rubble

A'a lava

Calendar stone, 3.5 m (11 ft) wide, carved by the Aztec people of Mexico

Gas bubble later filled with minerals such as silica or calcite

TYPES OF LAVA

As volcanoes explode, magma either blows apart as tiny ash particles or seeps out as red-hot lava flow. This lava can be of different kinds.

A'a lava
Thick a'a lava breaks into jagged blocks that cool and then ride on top of the lava flow.

Pahoehoe lava
Runny "pahoehoe" lava moves like candle wax. Its surface cools into a solid skin that buckles.

Pillow lava
Basalt erupted underwater forms rounded "pillows". The front of the pillow cools as it hits the water.

Mysterious mushroom stones carved by Central America's Mayan people more than 1,000 years ago

Mayan sculpture

Amygdaloidal basalt

A dark stone made up of fine crystal grains, basalt is the most common extrusive igneous (volcanic) rock on the planet. It pours out of volcanoes under the seas at mid-ocean ridges and forms the bulk of Earth's oceanic crust.

Although most of Earth's **basalt volcanoes** are below water, several are on the surface. The volcanoes of Hawaiian Islands and the African Rift Valley are basaltic "shield volcanoes". They create huge quantities of lava. Eruptions in India around 66 million years ago covered 1.5 million

Basalt lava bomb

Sharpened basalt blade on a modern woodworking tool

Hawaiian adze

Temple at Ellora Caves, India

Temples carved out of solid basalt

Iron-containing minerals in the basalt turn red as they rust

Head of Yarim-Lim

The **tallest basalt** columns at Giant's Causeway stand **12 m (39 ft)**.

The largest lava plateau in Europe, Giant's Causeway consists of 40,000 basalt columns

Giant's Causeway, Ireland

Carved bust in dark basalt of ancient Persian king, c. 1785 BCE

Axe or digging tool from Pueblo culture, southern USA, 750–900 CE

Lunar basalt rock

"Mare basalt" sample brought back from the Moon

sq km (0.6 million sq miles) to a depth of 2 km (1.2 miles). At **Ellora**, 34 majestic temples and monasteries have been carved out of the very same lava flow. Basalt volcanoes produce different types of lava (see box), including **a'a lava**. They also throw out bubbly **vesicular basalt** and **lava bombs**. On land, basalt lava forms hexagonal columns as it cools and cracks. **Giant's Causeway** in Ireland is a classic example. The dark patches on the Moon are **lunar basalt** – lava flows that date back to after the Moon formed in a giant asteroid smash with Earth.

VIOLENT EARTH
Kilauea Volcano on Big Island, Hawaii, erupts in a frenzy of red-hot lava and rage. Its fiery central crater is the mythical home of Pele, the Hawaiian fire goddess. Kilauea is one of the world's most active volcanoes and has been erupting continually since 1983. It produces a runny basalt lava, which pours out of the crater and the vents along the sides of the volcano and flows over the island to the sea.

Volcanoes are a vital part of the planet's rock cycle. Fed from magma chambers below Earth's surface, they recycle old rocks, and create new igneous rocks. Most volcanoes sit close to the margins of Earth's tectonic plates, points at which the edges of Earth's crust grind and bump against each other. Hawaii's volcanoes, however, sit plumb in the middle of the Pacific plate. Scientists think these volcanoes form as the plate inches slowly over the top of a "hot spot" in the underlying mantle. The volcano may have started out life 300,000–600,000 years ago, far beneath the waves. It grew and grew until, around 50,000 years ago, it finally emerged from the sea.

Metamorphic rocks

Band of granite rock

Migmatite

Fine grain size

Rock *has snakeskin texture*

Serpentinite

Slate

Splits *easily into thin sheets*

Marble

Amphibolite

Slate roof

Interlocking *grains of calcite*

Coarse-textured rock

Alternate *light and dark layers*

Gneiss

Red garnet crystals

Skarn

Dark band of minerals

Earth is not a quiet, calm planet. Its outer crust turns itself over, replacing, recycling, and renewing itself endlessly. Rocks caught in this churning mill are squeezed and heated until they turn into new metamorphic rocks.

Metamorphic rocks are shapeshifters – transformed from igneous and sedimentary rocks by heat and pressure underground. Pressure within the planet builds as it shifts and buckles. These stresses push on mineral crystals within the rocks, forcing them to align

Soft soapstone is easy to carve and polish

Composed mostly of the soft mineral talc

Soapstone

Soapstone scarab

Empty cone where sand was vaporized by lightning

Fulgurite

Recrystallization of minerals forms wavy patterns

Metaquartzite

Mylonite

Contains over 90 per cent quartz

Fulgurite is lightning **"frozen in stone"** at temperatures of 1,800°C (3,272°F).

Eclogite

Schist

Partially melted sand

Silvery colour comes from muscovite mica

into discrete layers. This turns mudstones into **slate**. Slate minerals are stacked up like the pages of a book, allowing them to break easily into flat sheets. Intense pressure also creates new minerals within the rock, forming the striped bands of **gneiss**. **Migmatites** have

recrystallized bands of granite swirling through them, while **eclogite** contains red garnets formed under extreme temperature and pressure. Intense pressure also creates **schist**, a flaky rock in which nearly all the mineral grains are parallel.

Marble

Green marble

Green colour comes from the mineral serpentine

Marble columns adorn the façade of this marvellous church in Lucca, Italy

San Michele church, Italy

Statue was carved from one big block of white marble

Statue of David

Marble made up of coarse crystals

White marble

Michelangelo's *David* is a **massive** nude, standing **5.17 m** (17 ft) tall.

Uncut marble

Veins of clay in original limestone rock

Marble pestle and mortar

Polished marble has waxy look

Marble is a metamorphic rock derived from limestone or dolomite. It is formed under the influence of extreme heat and pressure. It is not as soft as its appearance would suggest. This beautiful rock has been much loved by artists and architects.

Marble's combination of toughness and good looks is a product of metamorphism. When carbonate rocks, such as limestone or dolomite, are heated and put under pressure inside Earth's crust, calcium carbonate minerals recrystallize. This creates interlocking grains that scatter light

Cipollino marble

Lazurite in marble

Semiprecious lapis lazuli mixed into marble

Marble column

Travertine marble

Calcium carbonate is common to both marble and antacid tablets, which ease indigestion

Antacid tablets

Epidote and chlorite minerals produce veins

Delicate bands are formed

Marble columns were a favourite classical design

Angular patterns on marble called a breccia

Marble breccia

Chess piece

Banded calcite is known as onyx marble

White marble cladding covers exterior

Taj Mahal, India

MIGHTY MARBLE

35 m (115 ft)

38 m (125 ft)

Taj Mahal dome

Statue of Christ the Redeemer

Massive dome
The Taj Mahal, India, is the most spectacular marble building in the world. At 35 m (115 ft) tall, its amazing marble dome is almost as tall as the statue of Christ the Redeemer, which towers over Rio de Janeiro, Brazil.

and give the rock its creamy appearance. The classic colour is seen in **white marble**, which is often shot through with dark veins, as seen in this **pestle and mortar**. Italian artist Michelangelo (1475–1564) loved Carrara marble, and carved his masterpiece **David** from it. Marble comes in a huge range of colours and textures. **Cipollino marble**, also known as "onion stone", has swirling bands of metamorphic minerals. **Travertine marble** comes from limestone deposited in hot springs, while **marble breccia** is a striking mix of rock fragments and marble cement.

Sedimentary rocks

Feldspathic gritstone

Around one-quarter of this rock is made up of feldspar minerals

Greywacke

Fine-grained matrix of sand deposited in sea

Micaceous sandstone

Iron oxide patches

Shale

Layers of shale visible

Angular fragments show that grains have not been transported far

Breccia is often found along **fault lines** in rocks.

Breccia

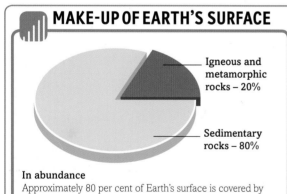

MAKE-UP OF EARTH'S SURFACE

Igneous and metamorphic rocks – 20%

Sedimentary rocks – 80%

In abundance
Approximately 80 per cent of Earth's surface is covered by sedimentary rocks. However, it is a very thin layer, as they barely make up one-tenth of the planet's crust.

When rain, wind, and weather beat against exposed rock, tiny grains wash away. Carried by streams and rivers, these sediments settle in thick beds at the bottom of lakes and oceans. Over time, minerals cement the grains together, forming sedimentary rock.

Sandstones are made from small grains of hard quartz. The mineral is tough and makes a hardwearing rock. All grains wear as they are moved, so the further sediments are transported, the smaller the grains and the rounder they are. **Breccia** is made from broken

Medium to coarse grains of sand and gravel

Gritstone

Puddingstone conglomerate

Large pebbles cemented together

Spectacular outcrop of 36 conglomerate domes in Australia's Northern Territory

Siltstone

Mudstone

No obvious layering on this hard and durable rock

Bricks are traditionally made with clay-rich rock

Bricks

Kata Tjuta domes, Australia

Fine-grained sediment

fragments of other rocks. Its grains are sharp and angular, rather than smooth and rounded. Coarse-grained **gritstone** is a sandstone renowned for its toughness – it was once used to make millstones for grinding wheat and sharpening tools. **Siltstone**, **shale**, and **mudstone** are all formed from fine particles of silt and clay. Mudstone has extremely fine grains that can only be seen with a microscope. Conglomerate rocks have the biggest grains of all. This **puddingstone conglomerate** has grains the size of cobblestones.

31

Limestone breccia

Grey, silica-rich fragments

Calcareous tufa

Nummulite fossils can grow as large as 5 cm (2 in)

Nummulitic limestone

Fossiliferous limestone

Fossilized shell embedded in a calcium carbonate matrix

Limestone mixed with muddy sediment

Strange shapes form when water evaporates

Marl

Soft, white powdery texture

Blackboard chalk

Chalk sticks are made of gypsum, although they were traditionally made from natural chalk

Red chalk

Sphinx, Egypt

Great Sphinx at Giza, Egypt, carved out of hillside of marl rock

Red colour comes from hematite

Clastic sedimentary rocks are composed of fragments of pre-existing materials. Certain **limestones** are formed from the remains of seashells and coral reefs. These are often full of fossils and make for a beautiful building stone. Hot springs and geysers deposit **tufa** limestone in weird shapes. **Nummulitic limestone** contains small round fossils called nummulites, but some sedimentary rocks are made entirely of fossils. **Chalk** is made of microscopic coccolith fossils, the remains of plankton algae. Although they are incredibly tiny, massed remains can build up into

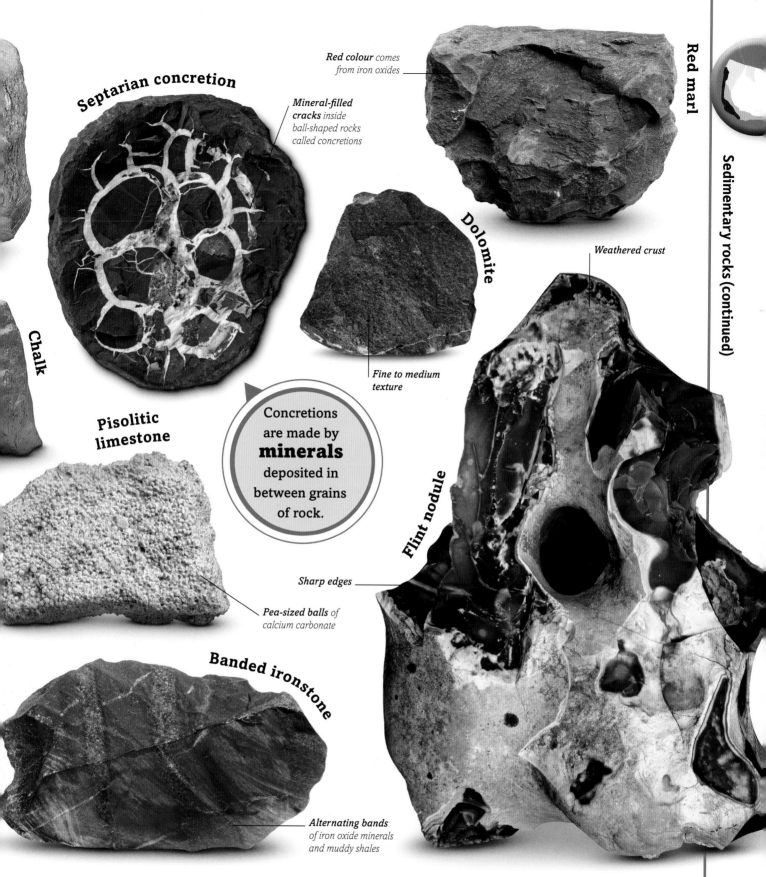

Red colour comes from iron oxides

Septarian concretion

Mineral-filled cracks inside ball-shaped rocks called concretions

Dolomite

Fine to medium texture

Weathered crust

Chalk

Concretions are made by **minerals** deposited in between grains of rock.

Pisolitic limestone

Flint nodule

Sharp edges

Pea-sized balls of calcium carbonate

Banded ironstone

Alternating bands of iron oxide minerals and muddy shales

vast white cliffs. Warm, shallow tropical seas roll calcium carbonate minerals into the little balls that make up **pisolitic limestones**. **Concretions** are rounded masses that form when waters circulating through rocks replace the cement minerals sticking sedimentary grains together.

Chemical sedimentary rocks develop when dissolved minerals form from water as solid grains. This process creates the iron-rich red bands in **ironstone**. **Flint** forms in hard nodules that break to give a sharp edge. Stone Age people used this to make tools.

33

Sandstone

Red colour due to iron oxide

Sandstone rock

Round grains

Red sandstone

Formed from wind-blown sand

Desert sandstone

The "four-faced Buddha" stands in Phnom Penh, Cambodia

Buddha statue

Sandstone elephants guard the entrance of Nathmalji-ki-Haveli mansion, India

Elephant statue

Greensand

Yellow colour comes from the blend of clear quartz and goethite

Yellow sandstone

Traditional sandstone bowl from Jaisalmer, India

Yellow sandstone bowl

Green colour due to presence of glauconite mica

A heap of sand is not a sedimentary rock. Sand turns into a hard stone as the individual grains are glued together with a mineral cement, such as silica or calcium carbonate. The classic sandstone rock is a tan, dun, or yellow colour.

Sandstones develop from fragments of other rocks. They are mostly composed of quartz and feldspars. The cement has a big influence on sandstone colour – **red sandstone** cement contains iron oxide. **Greensands** are greenish sandstones containing glauconite mica. **Desert**

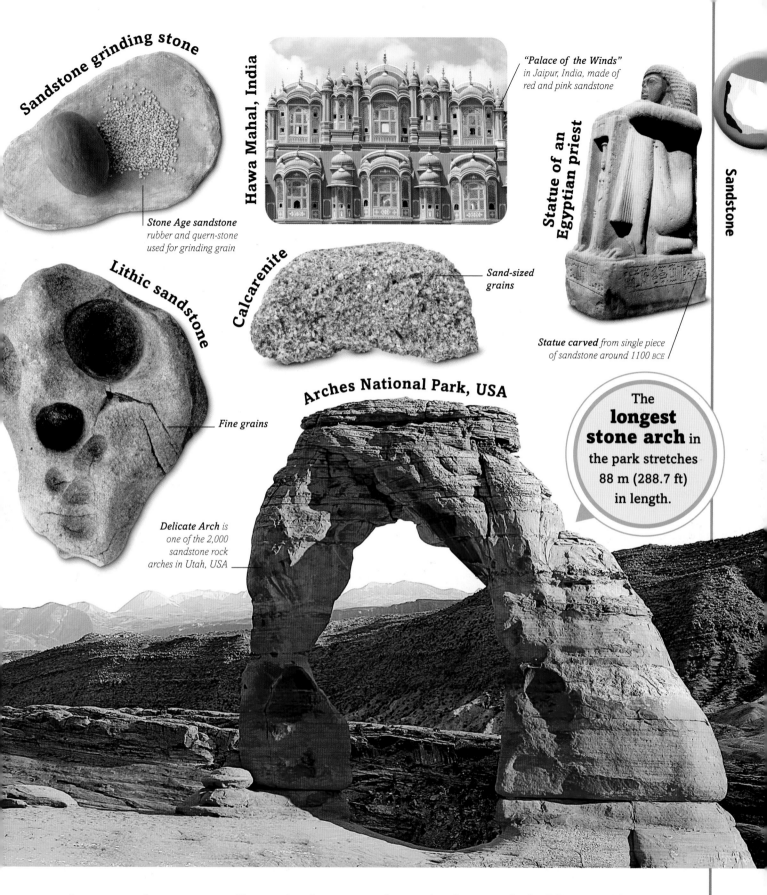

Sandstone grinding stone

Stone Age sandstone rubber and quern-stone used for grinding grain

Hawa Mahal, India

"Palace of the Winds" in Jaipur, India, made of red and pink sandstone

Statue of an Egyptian priest

Sand-sized grains

Sandstone

Statue carved from single piece of sandstone around 1100 BCE

Lithic sandstone

Calcarenite

Fine grains

Arches National Park, USA

Delicate Arch is one of the 2,000 sandstone rock arches in Utah, USA

The **longest stone arch** in the park stretches 88 m (288.7 ft) in length.

sandstone can be coarse- or fine-grained, while **lithic sandstones** contain lots of poorly sorted rock fragments. **Calcarenite** is a carbonate (limestone) type of sandstone, made up of sand-sized carbonate grains. Sandstone carves well and is used to make ornaments and decorative features for buildings and has been a popular material for making statues. Perhaps its most common use, however, is as a building stone. Some of the world's most iconic buildings, such as the **Hawa Mahal** palace in Jaipur, India, are made from sandstone blocks.

RAINBOW MOUNTAINS
These candy-striped mountains may look like an optical illusion but they actually consist of sandstone rock, built up by layer after layer of blue-grey, magenta, maroon, and lemon-coloured stone. One of the most beautiful landforms in China, they form part of the Zhangye Danxia Geological Park in Gansu Province, in the northwest of the country.

The sandstones of Gansu were deposited around 80 million years ago. Originally, the sediments would have settled on the beds of rivers and lakes, forming horizontal layers that lay one on top of the other. However, mighty changes were happening far to the south, as the Indian subcontinent ploughed into the Eurasian plate, crumpling and heaving up Earth's crust to create the Himalayan plateau. About 23 million years ago, these disturbances lifted up the Chinese sandstone beds and tilted them on their sides. Rain and water then eroded them, carving out hills. This weathering process created spectacular colours as different minerals in the sandstone reacted in different ways. The end result is a stunningly unique landscape.

Rocks from outer space

Hoba meteorite

This massive lump of iron crashed down in Namibia 80,000 years ago

Crosshatched mineral pattern of iron-nickel crystals

Iron meteorite

This rock fell to Earth about 13,000 years ago

Martian meteorite

Iron-nickel mixture resistant to weathering

Achondrite

Rock from the surface of an asteroid

Formed when a large meteorite smashed into Earth

Polished tektite

Green moldavite formed in meteorite impacts

Stony-iron meteorite

Tektite

Meteorite ring

Meteorite cut for jewellery

Look up to the sky on a clear night and you may see a shooting star. **More than 100 tonnes of dust and rocky fragments blaze in from space every day. They heat up as they punch through Earth's atmosphere and most of them burn away with a streak of light.**

Some space rocks called meteoroids enter Earth's atmosphere and burn up, creating a streak of light known as **meteor**. The meteoroids that survive and land on the ground are called **meteorites**. These are of three types – **iron**, **stony-iron**, and **stony meteorites**. Iron meteorites are almost pure iron,

Chondrite

Rounded silicate grains

Moon rock

Rock fragment *blasted off the Moon by meteorite impact*

Grey iron-nickel groundmass

Most **meteoroids** are about **4.5 billion years old**.

Meteor shower

Meteor showers happen when a cloud of debris left by a passing comet hits Earth's atmosphere

The Iron Man statue

Beads made from iron meteorite

Gerzeh beads

Statue carved from the Chinga meteorite that fell to Earth 15,000 years ago

Stony meteorite

Dull interior mostly made up of olivine and pyroxene minerals

COMET 67P

4,000 m (13,123 ft)

Comet 67P

3,776 m (12,388 ft)

Mount Fuji

Chasing space rocks
This 4-km- (2.4-mile-) tall comet is bigger than Mount Fuji in Japan. A space probe landed on its surface in 2014. It was the first such landing in history.

mixed with nickel. Weighing 60,000 tonnes, **Hoba meteorite**, in Namibia, is the largest example ever found. The **Gerzeh beads**, made by the ancient Egyptians, are also thought to be made of iron meteorite since the people of that time had not developed the smelting techniques required to separate iron from its mineral ore. A group of meteorites are thought to have come from Mars. These are called **Martian meteorites**. Stony-iron meteorites are the most common. They come from near the cores of large asteroids. Achondrites and chondrites are two types of stony meteorites.

IMPACT CRATER
Gosse's Bluff is a massive meteor crater in Australia's Central Desert. Known by the Aboriginal name "Tnorala", this scar on the landscape records the moment when a giant object came crashing out of the skies and collided with Earth's surface. Interestingly, both Aboriginal and scientific explanations as to how the Bluff was formed are very similar.

According to the traditional Aborigine story, at the dawn of time a group of women danced across the sky, creating the Milky Way as they twisted and twirled. One of the mothers put her baby down to rest, but the cradle toppled out of the sky and crashed to Earth, creating the hollow of Tnorala, surrounded by circular rock walls. Scientists believe that, around 143 million years ago, a meteoroid blazed in from outer space on a collision course with our planet. It smashed into the surface, blasting a crater 20 km (12.4 miles) across. Today only the central part of this vast crater remains in the middle of the desert. It is up to 5 km (3 miles) in diameter.

MINERALS AND GEMS

Minerals and gems

Minerals are the basic building blocks of solid Earth. All rocks are made out of tiny, mixed mineral grains. Each mineral has a definite chemical recipe, and can be identified by its crystal form (known as its habit), colour, hardness, surface shine (lustre), and the way in which it breaks. Gems are cut and polished mineral crystals. These stones are highly prized for their beauty and rarity.

Naturally occurring mineral ›
Minerals are naturally occurring solids. Some form solid crystals as molten liquid rock cools; others crystallize out of fluids loaded with dissolved minerals trickling through the rocks.

Amethyst

Single amethyst crystal

Mineral crystal ❯ A definite chemical composition and an ordered internal arrangement of atoms gives minerals the flat faces and sharp edges of crystals.

Oval mixed-cut amethyst

Cut gem ❯ Gems are exceptionally beautiful crystals that are shaped and polished to enhance their appearance.

Rich purple colour due to traces of iron and radiation

Agate base

Crystal systems

Crystals can be divided into six groups based on their shape.

Tetragonal
• Have three axes of symmetry, all at right angles, two of which are of equal length.

Orthorhombic
• Similar to monoclinic system, but all three axes are at right angles. Habits are tabular and prismatic.

Monoclinic
• Have three unequal axes of symmetry, only two at right angles. Tabular and prismatic shapes are common.

Trigonal/hexagonal
• Both systems are similar, with four axes of symmetry. Crystals are often six-sided with tops like a pyramid.

Cubic
• Are common and easily recognized. Have three axes at right angles, and shapes can be four- or eight-sided.

Triclinic
• Have a low degree of symmetry, because three axes are unequal in length and are not at right angles.

CARATS

A carat is the standard measure of weight for precious stones and metals. One carat is equal to 0.2 g (0.007 oz). It is also used as a measure of the purity of gold – pure gold being 24 carats (4.8 g/0.16 oz).

Native minerals

Iron

Stony meteorite contains nickel-iron

Antimony

Brittleness of antimony gives it a flaky texture

Platinum

Nuggets of platinum are rare

Rich, white lustre

Platinum rings

Sulfur

Distinctive yellow crystals

Sulfur containing mercaptan is added to gas supplies to **detect leaks**.

Most minerals are made of two or more chemical elements bonded together. A small handful, however, are not combined with anything else and are found in their natural, or "native", state. Some of these minerals are highly valued precious metals.

Gold is the most highly prized of all metals and is so unreactive that it is typically found in a relatively pure form. It is used to make ornaments, jewellery, money, and for numerous industrial applications. **Platinum** is usually found in its native metallic form in alloys. The metal is often

46

Copper

Copper *can be easily shaped into vessels like this kettle*

Copper kettle

Crystalline copper has a distinctive red-brown colour

COPPER GIANTS

Top producers of copper
One of the most important metals, copper is found in ores all over the world. In 2014, Chile was the largest producer of copper.

Values in 1,000 tonnes

| 5,800 | 1,614 | 1,368 | 1,339 | 961 |

Key
Chile
China
USA
Peru
Australia

Pencil lead *is made of soft graphite*

Graphite lead

Graphite

Crystal form of carbon

Diamond

Bismuth

Crystals are slablike and shiny

Soft and greasy to the touch

Arsenic is **highly poisonous** to **humans**.

Mineral shape is "botryoidal", or like a cluster of grapes

Arsenic

Gold

Silver

Nugget weighs about 2.5 kg (5.5 lb)

Native silver can look like a mass of twisted wires

used to make jewellery. **Copper** and **silver** are usually found combined with other minerals. Native **iron** is found in weathered iron ore deposits or arrives on Earth in meteorites from space. Bright yellow crystals of native **sulfur** are found around volcanoes and hot springs. These crystals are used in the production of sulfuric acid – one of the most important industrial chemicals. The element carbon is found in two forms: **diamond** is the hardest known mineral in the world; while **graphite** is a soft, greasy mineral that has many different uses.

Gold

Delicate details on Egyptian necklace from 4th century BCE

Ancient gold necklace

Gold crystals

Tiny crystals

Gold grains

Gold nugget

Solid lump

Grains are 1–4 mm (0.03–0.15 in) thick

Tutankhamen's burial mask

Flat gold plates

Egyptian pharaoh's burial mask has kept its soft sheen for more than 3,000 years

Thin scales of gold embedded in quartz-rich rock

Gold is the most sought-after mineral known to man. Its beauty and rarity make this precious metal valuable. Gold keeps its soft, yellow sheen because it does not corrode or tarnish easily.

Although some lucky people find **gold nuggets** or **crystals**, most gold is found as flakes or **grains** in river silt, where it has washed out of rocks. It is taken out from these deposits by "panning" – washing the silt through a sieve. Throughout history,

Gold coins

British sovereign coins

The **largest gold nugget** ever found weighed 71 kg (156.5 lb).

Intricate design in gold leaf

Gold leaf

RARE RESOURCE

Total amount of gold mined in history would make a solid ball 24 m (78.7 ft) across – the length of a tennis court.

The hunt for gold

An estimated 183,600 tonnes of gold have been mined in human history – around 80 per cent of Earth's total reserves of gold.

Ceremonial gold cup from Chimú culture (1100–1470), in modern-day Peru

Gold medal

XX. Olympiade München 1972

Ram's head engraved in gold

Medieval signet ring

Chimú cup

Medal from the 1972 Olympic Games

367432

Gold bullion

Superthin layer of gold on visor

Satellite parts

Astronaut's visor

Gold covering

Bars of solid gold weighing 1 kg (2.2 lb) each

the sight of even a small speck of gold has been enough to spark a gold rush. It has been used for centuries as a store of wealth – as **jewellery**, **coins**, or **gold bullion**. An Olympic **gold medal**, such as this one from the 1972 Summer Olympic Games in Munich, West Germany, is made of 92.5 per cent silver with a thin coating of 6 g (0.2 oz) of gold. A thin layer of gold on an **astronaut's visor** provides protection from the Sun's glare and heat. Gold foil is used to cover **satellites** as it keeps out harmful radiation.

Silver

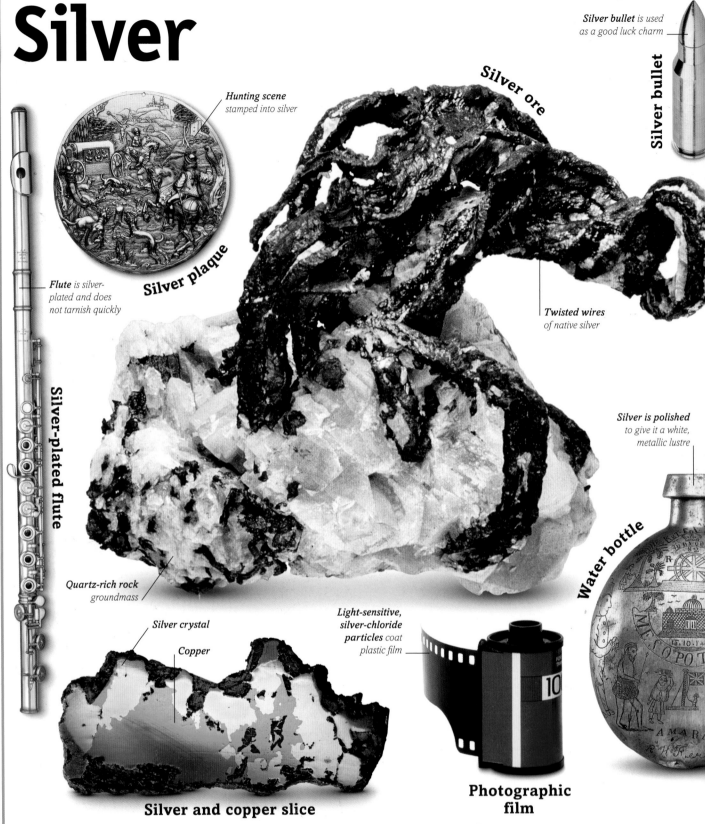

Silver bullet is used as a good luck charm

Silver bullet

Silver ore

Hunting scene stamped into silver

Silver plaque

Flute is silver-plated and does not tarnish quickly

Silver-plated flute

Twisted wires of native silver

Silver is polished to give it a white, metallic lustre

Water bottle

Quartz-rich rock groundmass

Silver crystal

Copper

Light-sensitive, silver-chloride particles coat plastic film

Silver and copper slice

Photographic film

Silver is a pale, beautifully shiny, precious metal. Found in our planet's crust as both an ore mineral and in its pure, native form, it has been mined since ancient times. However, unlike gold, silver nuggets are very rare.

Although most silver is found in ores, native silver forms as crystals and as attractive twisted **wires** in rocks. Silver is highly prized as a decorative metal, and is used for jewellery and **coins**. Ancient Greek "tetradrachm" coins and ancient Roman "denarii" are hugely valuable collector's

Native silver

Embossed
design on mirror

Solar panel

Silver mirror

Pure silver crystal

Silver paste
conducts electricity
out of solar cells

Wire silver

Silver guard worn
to protect fingernails

Edible silver foil on sweets

Nail protector

Bent and twisted
"fingers" of wire silver

Silver "vark" covering
Indian mithai, or sweets

One
million **cell
phones** contain
about **350 kg
(772 lb)**
of silver.

STERLING SILVER

92.5% silver

Silver coin

Silver paint used
on electronic circuit

Circuit board

7.5% copper

Popular alloy
Jewellery and silverware are traditionally
made from sterling silver. This alloy contains
a mix of silver (92.5 per cent) and copper
(7.5 per cent).

Ancient Greek coin
from 5th century BCE

items. High-quality musical instruments, such as
flutes and trumpets, are made of silver alloy or
silver-plated metal. In legend, **silver bullets** kill
werewolves, but despite its mythical power, the
metal is rather too expensive for bullets. Silver
was once an active ingredient in **photographic**
film, but digital cameras have made it a thing
of the past. **Silver foil** just micrometres thick,
called "vark", is sometimes used to cover sweets
or other food items. Silver is also a natural
conductor of electricity, and is used in
circuit boards and **solar panels**.

Diamond

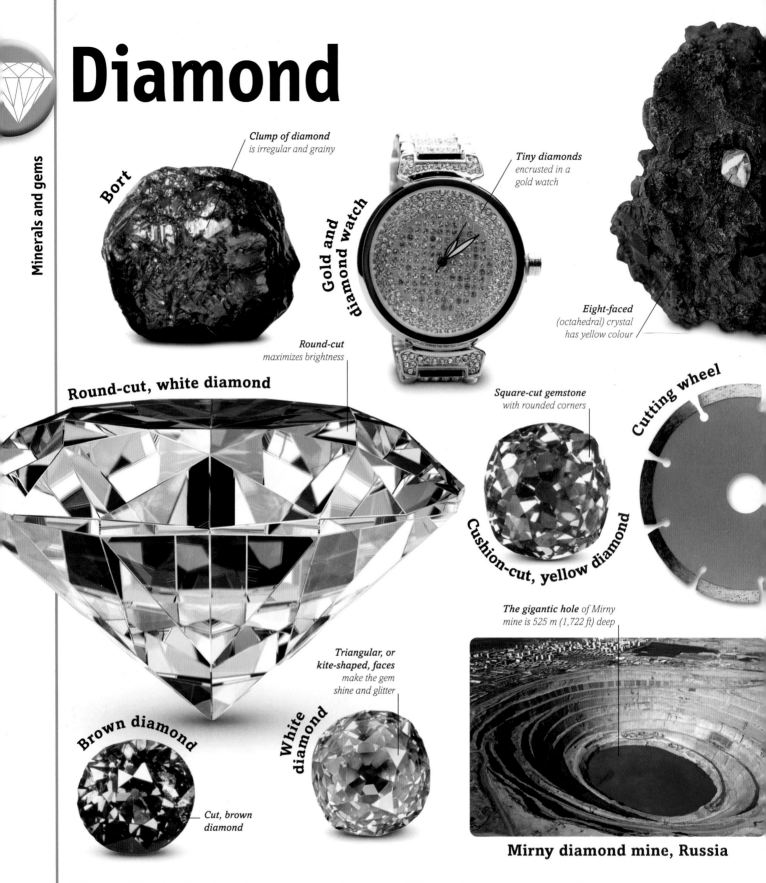

Bort

Clump of diamond is irregular and grainy

Gold and diamond watch

Tiny diamonds encrusted in a gold watch

Eight-faced (octahedral) crystal has yellow colour

Round-cut, white diamond

Round-cut maximizes brightness

Square-cut gemstone with rounded corners

Cutting wheel

Cushion-cut, yellow diamond

The gigantic hole of Mirny mine is 525 m (1,722 ft) deep

Brown diamond

Cut, brown diamond

White diamond

Triangular, or kite-shaped, faces make the gem shine and glitter

Mirny diamond mine, Russia

Diamond is the hardest known material in the world. It is lustrous, bright, and resistant to dulling or scratching. Diamonds are formed in Earth's mantle, 140–190 km (87–118 miles) underground. They make beautiful gems and are highly desirable.

Diamonds are so precious that they are used almost exclusively for jewellery – inlaid in **watches**, worn as **earrings**, or set in **rings**. Most diamonds are slightly yellow to brown, due to nitrogen impurities or other defects. Pure diamonds are colourless. One of the most famous

Rough diamond embedded in kimberlite

Diamond necklace

Pear-shaped diamond

Glass-cutting tool

Small diamond set in the tip of cutting tool

Diamond ring

Cluster diamond on engagement ring

Marie Antoinette's earrings

Large, pear-shaped diamonds that once belonged to the French Queen

The **Koh-i-Noor** diamond was recut in 1852 to make a **105.6-carat** stone.

Hope Diamond

Blue colour caused by tiny amounts of boron

Diamonds embedded around the edge of grinding wheel

Powdered diamond on head of tool can cut gem diamonds

Koh-i-Noor diamond

Diamond-coated tools

Queen Mother's crown

GIANT GEM

Cullinan Diamond

10 cm (4 in)

Record breaker

The Cullinan Diamond, discovered in 1905 in South Africa, was twice the size of any other diamond ever found. It was split into 9 large pieces and 96 smaller stones.

gems, the **Hope Diamond**, is a beautiful deep blue. Not all diamonds are precious. **Bort** is an industrial grade, non-gem diamond that is crushed to make **cutting tools** and **wheels**. Diamonds reach the planet's surface by being carried by molten rock in special volcanic eruptions that originated deep in Earth. They are also found embedded in certain types of igneous rock. Sites where these rocks are found can be mined, such as the **Mirny diamond mine** in Russia. They are also found in gravel deposits in river beds, because the rock around them has been eroded by the water.

Copper

Bronze statue, in St Petersburg, Russia, sits on what is thought to be the largest boulder ever moved by humans

Bronze Horseman

Fingerlike crystals of pure copper

Cuprite crystal

Cuprite

Native copper

Chalcopyrite

Crystals normally have triangular shape

Malachite

Copper is easily shaped with a hammer

Copper jug

Growth rings inside a malachite stalactite

COPPER CRYSTAL

Largest copper mass *(420 tonnes)*	School bus *(Weight of 42 buses: 420 tonnes)*

Copper giant
The largest single chunk of native copper ever found was in Michigan, USA, in 1857. It weighed 420 tonnes, as much as 42 school buses.

Brass bells

Bright brass is an alloy of copper and zinc

Wire carries electrical current

Copper wire

Copper is a metal element that has been used since ancient times. Soft and easily shaped, this metal forms a variety of useful alloys when mixed with other metals. It is an excellent conductor of electricity and is used to carry electrical current.

This reddish-brown metal is found as a native mineral or is extracted from its many ores. **Malachite** was the very first copper ore mined. Although the oxide mineral **cuprite** contains much more copper, it was easier to extract from malachite. **Chalcopyrite** is the most important

Bronze
helmet

Roman gladiator's
"galea" (helmet)

Electric
motor coil

Copper bars

Copper
plumbing pipes

Sharp bronze tip

Nebra Sky Disc

Pipe carries water
supply in the home

Green "verdigris" weathering
forms on copper surfaces

Bronze Age
spearhead

Bronze disc inlaid
with gold stars,
Sun, and Moon

Large
chalcocite crystal

Chalcocite

Statue of Liberty

Around
91 tonnes of
copper sheets were
used to make
this statue.

Copper coin

Coin is made of
copper-plated zinc

ore today. Although it has a lower copper content, it occurs in vast deposits and the copper can be easily extracted. Copper mixed with tin makes bronze. Discovered around 2500 BCE, bronze is tougher than pure copper. In the Bronze Age, people used it to make swords, **helmets**, and **spearheads**. The **Nebra Sky Disc**, from Germany, is a 3,600-year-old sky map made of bronze. Today, copper is used for roofing and for making **pipes**, **wire**, electronic components, energy-efficient motors, and **coins**. The **Statue of Liberty** is the world's largest copper statue.

MIGHTY MINE
In open-pit mining, the land covering a deposit of mineral ores is removed and an immense hollow is gouged into the ground to extract the metal-containing rocks. This results in the world's deepest man-made holes, some of which are visible from space. To limit the danger of rock falls, a series of steps are dug into the walls of the mines.

The Morenci mine in Arizona, USA, first opened in 1872, is one of the world's largest open-pit copper mines. Reserves of an estimated 3.2 billion tonnes of copper ore lie in these hills, in copper porphyry deposits. The excavation is undertaken on a giant scale. Dynamite blasts apart the pit's steep, stepped sides, loosening entire hillsides of rock. Then, gigantic, bucket-wheel excavating machines move in, taking huge bites of earth and stone, and loading them into monster trucks. The copper ore is taken to a mill, where it is crushed into a fine powder. The mine produces over 380,000 tonnes of copper every year and employs approximately 2,000 people.

Sulfides

Metallic lustre of *molybdenite crystals*

Molybdenite

Ring inlaid with small iron pyrite crystals

Chalk groundmass

Pyrite ring

Crystals are silvery-yellow colour

Copper ingot

dh
10-0z
Fine Copper

Marcasite

Pure copper extracted by smelting copper ore in a furnace

Galena

Cubic crystal

Copper ore

GIANT GALENA

25 cm (9.8 in)
25 cm (9.8 in)

Colossal crystal
The largest galena crystal ever reported is a cube with sides measuring 25 cm (9.8 in). It was found in the Great Laxey Mine, Isle of Man, UK.

Yellow chalcopyrite

Among the most important metal ores in the world, sulfides are a group of commonly dark, dense minerals made of sulfur combined with metal. Sulfides do not usually make good gemstones because they are too soft.

Galena is a typical sulfide mineral. Soft, shiny, and heavy, this sulfide forms striking six-faced (cubic) or eight-faced (octahedral) crystals. Galena, one of the main sources of lead, is often found alongside other ores, such as marcasite, **pyrite**, **chalcopyrite**, and sphalerite. Marcasite,

Covellite

Crystals form in thin planes

Octahedral crystals

Hauerite

Millerite

Calcite groundmass

Hexagonal (six-sided) crystals with a bronze-metallic lustre

Chalcopyrite with quartz crystals

Pyrrhotite

Needles of brassy-yellow millerite contain nickel

Transparent, colourless quartz crystal

Cinnabar

Brassy, metallic chalcopyrite crystal

Purple, oxidized bornite

Chalcocite

Copper is the **third-most-used metal** in industries around the world.

Mineral formed in grains

Lead-grey colour

an iron ore, shares the same composition as pyrite, but it has a different structure. **Cinnabar** is an unusual, brightly coloured sulfide. It is the principal ore of mercury, and sometimes releases beads of the liquid metal. Indigo-blue **covellite** is a copper ore, first found on the famous volcano Mount Vesuvius in Italy. Purple **copper ore**, also called peacock ore, is one of the most colourful minerals in the world. This mix of bornite and chalcopyrite minerals can form dull **chalcocite**, another ore mineral that has the highest copper content of perhaps all sulfides.

59

Pyrite

Cubic crystals

Rock groundmass

Made of zinc, which comes from sphalerite

Watering can

Sphalerite is the **most common** ore of **zinc**.

Rare, prismatic realgar crystal

Sphalerite

Needlelike crystals

Crystal face has vertical grooves

Proustite

Crystal has golden-brown colour

White dolomite

Crystals are ruby red

Some sulfide minerals masquerade as other minerals and are easily misidentified. **Pyrite** is the most notorious – it is also known as "fool's gold" and "brazzle" because its dazzling shine can fool the unwary into thinking they have found pure gold. Fool's gold, however, contains no real gold, just iron and sulfur. It is harder and more brittle than gold and is less dense. **Sphalerite** can also deceive the unwary. This mineral has several different forms and contains zinc. **Nickeline** is rarely used as a source of nickel because it often contains the deadly poison

Realgar

Glaucodot

Bournonite

Quartz groundmass

Sharp-edged *prismatic crystal with metallic lustre*

Prismatic crystal *contains cobalt, iron, and arsenic with sulfur*

Tennantite

Powdered orpiment

Golden pigment *is called "king's yellow"*

Pyrargyrite

Jamesonite

Crystals *are steel-grey colour*

Patches *of copper-red lustre*

Orpiment

Rock groundmass

Dark, twinned, prismatic crystals

Nickeline

Stibnite

Surface lustre *gives the appearance of a resin*

The Germans called nickeline, ***"copper nickel"*** though it contains no copper.

Prismatic crystals *are long and heavily grooved*

arsenic. **Realgar** is sometimes called "ruby sulfur", and it is a soft mineral that crumbles easily. Its partner in crime is **orpiment**. Both of these minerals form around volcanic vents, were once used to make paint pigments, and also contain arsenic. Sometimes associated with realgar and galena, **stibnite** is the principal ore of the metal antimony. Sulfosalts are a rare group of minerals that contain a metal and a semimetal, such as arsenic. **Proustite**, also called ruby silver, and **pyrargyrite** are important sources of silver.

Pyrite

Octahedral pyrite

Radiating needle of quartz

Perfect octahedron

Grooves, called **striations**, *show how the mineral grew in layers*

Pyrite is the most **abundant** sulfide mineral in Earth's crust.

Cubic pyrite

Cubic crystals intersect to form crosses

Pyrite cross

Nodular pyrite

Tiny crystals

Cubic pyrite crystal

Fool's gold

Brass-yellow crystal with bright, metallic lustre

Pyrite cubes

Pyrite is a bright and shiny pretender. If you are not careful, it will trick you into thinking that you have struck gold. However, pyrite will not make you rich. It contains nothing of value, except, perhaps, some iron.

Pyrite gets its name from the Greek word "pyr", meaning "fire", because pyrite emits sparks when struck by iron. Its gleaming gold crystals of pyrite are known as "**fool's gold**" because of their power to dazzle. However, it is easy to tell the difference between the precious metal and

Wheellock rifle

Firing mechanism uses a piece of pyrite

Pyritized ammonite fossil

Pyrite was one of the first minerals to be mined here

Rio Tinto mines, Spain

Pyrite replaces shell's minerals during fossilization

Sulfuric acid

H_2SO_4 KOH

Important industrial chemical made with pyrite

Dodecahedral pyrite

Pyrite nodules

Hard, spherical mass

Pyrite sun discs

Radiating crystals inside a pyrite nodule

Crystal faces are of different sizes, unlike a regular dodecahedron

this worthless iron sulfide. Pyrite is less dense and harder than gold and forms perfect cubic crystals. Another test is to scrape the mineral down a scratch plate, as pyrite leaves a streak of greenish-black powder, rather than flakes of gold. As well as cubes and **octahedrons** (eight-faced shapes),

pyrite forms **dodecahedron** crystals with 12 faces. It also forms **nodules**, some of which have radiating crystals inside. Pyrite is used to make **sulfuric acid** and because it makes sparks when struck, it was also used to ignite gunpowder in **wheellock rifles**.

Ore minerals

Long, prismatic crystals *sometimes form as needles*

Rutile

Salt

Salt is a source of lithium

Energy-saving light

X-ray image reveals tubes of mercury vapour

Tiny, red crystals contain mercury

Cinnabar

Cinnabar takes its name from the Arabic for **"dragon blood"**.

White calcite

Lightweight, rechargeable battery

LITHIUM ION BATTERY
Li-ion 3.7V 1600mAh
Charge limit voltage 4.2v
Standard GB-18287-2000
Production Date: 2009.12
Attention: 1 Do not approach the fire to avoid detonation
2 Do not disassemble the battery secretly
3 Strictly prohibit short circuiting
4 Please refer to the user handbook when the
battery need charging

Lithium ion battery

Pea-sized, mineral grains in aluminium oxide groundmass

Bauxite

Cassiterite

Metallic yellow colour with bronzelike tarnish

Dull lustre

Uraninite

Prismatic crystals, rich in tin

Ores are minerals that contain valuable metals in large enough amounts to be worth mining. Many of them are oxides and sulfides, and contain oxygen or sulfur. Ores are mined and then refined to extract the metals they carry.

Important metals such as iron and copper are extracted from their ores in a chemical process called smelting, which requires high temperatures. The three main iron ores are the oxides hematite, **magnetite**, and ilmenite. Iron is often turned into steel, which is used in the construction

Bornite

Coppery brown colour

Cobaltite

Cubelike crystal with metallic sheen

Magnetite

Fluorite

Zones of purple and green colour

Pentlandite

Cluster of black magnetite crystals

Shiny, nickel plating is cheaper and more durable than chrome. Pentlandite is a major ore of nickel.

Nickel-plated motorcycle

BINGHAM CANYON MINE

Bingham Canyon Mine

1,000 m (3,300 ft)

Empire State Building 443 m (1,454 ft)

Largest manmade hole
The Bingham Canyon Mine in Utah, USA, is an open-pit copper mine, nearly 1 km (0.6 mile) deep. Two Empire State Buildings stacked on top of each other inside it would not even reach the top.

industry to build skyscrapers and bridges. **Bornite**, a major source of copper, is also called a "peacock ore" because of its multicoloured appearance. **Rutile** is a source of titanium, a light, strong metal, often used to make aircraft parts and added to steel to make it stronger.

Uraninite is refined to produce uranium, the metal that is used to power a nuclear reactor. **Bauxite** is the main source of aluminium. As well as being a source of fluorine, **fluorite** is also used during smelting, helping to speed up the process.

Oxides

Microlite

Crystal containing tantalum

Octahedral crystal

Crystal face has bright, glossy lustre

Franklinite

Jet-black franklinite crystal in calcite groundmass

Shiny, metallic lustre

Cassiterite

Crystal can form as fine fibres

Pyrolusite

Manganese forms part of alkaline batteries. Pyrolusite is a common manganese mineral.

Button cell batteries

Many minerals contain oxygen, but oxide minerals are specifically those formed by one or more elements teamed with oxygen. Oxides are often stunning, and this group features some of the most gorgeous, glittering gemstones.

Many oxides are important ores of metals because they contain metal elements in their crystals. **Cuprite** is a source of copper, while uranium is extracted from **uraninite**. **Pyrolusite**, the most common ore of manganese, forms in lumps as well as in fibrous crystals. **Spinel** is the

Gahnite

Varlamoffite

Varlamoffite crystals

Crystal has octahedral shape

Pyrochlore

"Secondary" tin oxide crystal formed by weathering

Uraninite

Spinel

Rutile

Needles of rutile embedded in "rutilated quartz"

Yellow uranium oxide

Rutile is a common titanium mineral

Mass of ruby-red crystals

Titanium watch

Uraninite is highly **radioactive** and must be handled with care.

Brookite

Tabular brookite crystal on a mass of smaller albite crystal

Crystal forms in veins of metamorphic rock

Anatase

Albite crystal

name for both a single mineral and for a group of more than 20 minerals. Blood-red spinels often get mistaken for rubies. The Black Prince's ruby, set into the British Imperial State Crown, is actually a 170-carat (34 g/1.2 oz) spinel the same size as a ping-pong ball. Zinc-containing **gahnite** is a brown-grey spinel, while iron-rich **franklinite** is black. **Brookite, rutile**, and **anatase** are titanium oxides that share identical chemical compositions, but have different atomic arrangements. Minerals containing tin are rare; **cassiterite** is the only known commercial source of tin.

Figurine carved from a single corundum crystal

Sapphire Buddha

Prismatic Kashmir ruby embedded in rocky groundmass

Corundum: ruby

The finest sapphires come from **Sri Lanka**, **Myanmar**, and **India**.

Colour distributed unevenly

Corundum: sapphire

Black ilmenite crystal

Sapphire variety of corundum in its rough form

Ilmenite

Chrysoberyl

Chromite

Nodule of chromite

GEMSTONE RECORD-BREAKER

56 mm (2.2 in) long

Black Star of Queensland sapphire

Hen's egg

Super sapphire
About the size of a hen's egg, the 733-carat (146.6 g/5.1 oz) Black Star of Queensland is the world's largest star sapphire.

Aluminium oxide may not sound exciting, but it forms no less than three highly prized gemstones. Pink and clear- to blue-coloured varieties of corundum are known as **sapphires**, while **rubies** are blood red. A third, pink-orange form, called "padparadscha", is even more rare.

Chrysoberyl is an aluminium oxide that also contains beryllium. Its most rare variety – a gem called alexandrite – changes colour under electric lighting. **Chromite** is the world's most important source of chromium. It is used to make gleaming, chrome-plated bathroom taps, car parts, and

Magnetite

Crystal has eight-sided (octahedral) shape

Chinese compass

Ancient compass crafted from lodestone

Trigonal hematite

Well-formed crystal with metallic lustre

Perovskite crystals look cubic but are slightly squashed to one side

Perovskite

Magnetite (lodestone)

Iron filings attracted to magnetite by its powerful magnetic forces

Hematite kidney ore

Rounded lump of ore with red iron-oxide weathering

Deep-red zincite

Zincite

Wedge-shaped, twinned crystal with a glassy lustre

kitchen appliances, and is also added to steel to make it super-hard. Chromite occurs in sedimentary layers or in weathered nodules within a rock. **Magnetite** is an iron oxide related to spinel. A naturally magnetic mineral, it is also known as **lodestone**. Magnetite and **hematite** are major ores of iron – a key ingredient of steel. **Ilmenite** is another black mineral, which resembles magnetite or hematite. It is an iron, titanium oxide, so is a major source of titanium, the wonder-metal with the highest strength-to-weight ratio of all metals.

Ice

Perito Moreno Glacier, Argentina

Iceberg floats in water, the liquid form of ice

Polar bear stranded on Arctic iceberg

Ice sawn and chiselled into this shape

Ice castle on Lake Louise, Canada

Blocks of ice break off, or calve, from front edge of glacier

Snowflake

Symmetrical, six-pointed pattern

Castle built on surface of frozen lake

Iceberg

Hubbard Glacier, Alaska, USA

Ice cores in freezer

Around 90 per cent of iceberg is under water

Tubes cut from ancient ice are stored for analysis

River of ice flows very slowly

Minerals are any natural solids with a definite crystal structure and ice is one of the most abundant minerals on Earth's surface. It exists naturally only in cold areas, such as on mountain peaks and in the polar regions, or as hail or snow.

Like iron ore, ruby, and cuprite, ice is also an oxide. Unlike the other oxides, however, it exists mostly in its liquid form, as water. As a solid, it is found as ice crystals (which form **snowflakes**, **glaciers**, and ice caps), **icicles**, hailstones, and frost. Most of the world's ice is in the polar regions. Antarctica

Halo effect

Glowing ring around Sun caused by ice crystals in atmosphere

Icicles

Dripping meltwater refreezes into long spikes

Huge chunk of ice can float for weeks on the ocean

Igloo

Temporary shelter built out of blocks cut from ice and covered in snow

Natural ice sculpture

Strange, curving shapes formed as the ice is melted by the Sun

The temperature at the **core** of an iceberg can be as low as **-20°C** (-4°F).

HUGE HAILSTONE

Tennis ball
6.8 cm (2.75 in)

Giant hailstone
20 cm (8 in)

Large ball
The largest hailstone ever seen fell in South Dakota, USA, in 2010. It measured 20 cm (8 in) across, roughly the size of three tennis balls.

is covered in a layer of ice about 2 km (1.2 mile) thick. The ice in this layer has been deposited over many thousands, if not millions, of years. Scientists drill into the ice to cut long, tube-shaped samples, called **ice cores**. These reveal what conditions on Earth were like in the past. In winter, most of the Arctic Ocean is covered in a 3–4-m- (9.8–13-ft-) thick sheet of ice, but much of this melts in summer, cracking up into giant **icebergs**. Snow houses called **igloos** are found in the Arctic region. Rivers of ice called **glaciers** move slowly down mountains, cutting valleys as they go.

UNDER THE ICE
An explorer stops to take in the wonder of an ice cave. Meltwater flowing underneath the Muir Glacier at Alaska's Glacier Bay National Park has carved a spectacular cavern. We do not often think of ice as a mineral, but it ticks all the boxes – it occurs naturally, is not formed by living things, is solid, and has a regular, internal crystal arrangement.

Ice occurs in vast deposits at Earth's poles – in fact, it is one of the most common minerals on the planet's surface. As snowfalls build up, ice crystals are compressed and compacted until they accumulate and form large, light blue-coloured masses. When it forms over land, ice can remain for thousands of years. In some places, an ice cap can be 2 km (1.2 miles) thick. Very few minerals can be said to last forever, but ice is particularly unstable – it turns into liquid water at temperatures over 0°C (32°F). In the Arctic, an expanse of sea ice the size of Australia melts every summer, but each winter sees less ice forming. As global temperatures rise, melting ice caps add water to the oceans, raising sea levels, and affecting global weather patterns.

Fluorescent minerals

Blue fluorescence produced by barium titanium silicate mineral

Wernerite, a common form of scapolite, glows a vivid green-yellow colour

Wernerite

Willemite and calcite

Benitoite

Delicate, violet blue glow is due to the presence of europium or other rare-earth elements

Fluorite

Sodalite

Benitoite was discovered by the **San Benito River** in California, USA.

Rock groundmass

Scapolite

Sodalite fluoresces a bright orange

Scapolite fluoresces yellow

A chunk of zinc ore looks plain in dull browns and black, but turn off the lights and flick on an ultraviolet (UV) lamp and it bursts into an array of bright colours. Known as "fluorescence", this phenomenon is common to all fluorescent minerals.

Many minerals sparkle and shimmer in wild colours when viewed under UV light. This "flourescent" effect gets its name from **fluorite** – the mineral in which it was first observed, in 1852. Lots of common minerals change their colours totally under UV light.

Calcite
fluoresces pink and red

Bright green fluorescence

Adamite

Willemite glows green

Gypsum fluoresces a cream colour

Gypsum

Quartz geode

The chalcedony variety of quartz deposited around the interior of a hollow in a rock

Aragonite

Salmon-pink glow given off by aragonite

Calcite

Brick-red glow is due to the presence of manganese

Adamite, a zinc arsenate, shines bright green. **Calcite**, one of the most abundant minerals on the planet, is normally colourless, but the crystals fluoresce a bright, deep orange. What is needed for this strange glow is an "activator" – an element whose atoms absorb the energy of UV light, and then re-emit it as visible light. A small amount of manganese acts as an activator for both **aragonite** and calcite. Iron, on the other hand, can be a "quencher", meaning that it suppresses fluorescence in some minerals.

Hydrated minerals

Howlite

Nodules of white howlite

Pisolitic bauxite

Rounded, pea-sized grain called a "pisolith"

Aluminium foil trays

Aluminium from bauxite is used to make a range of kitchen foil products

Brucite

Tabular crystals in rock groundmass

Manganite

Dark manganite crystal contains the metal manganese

Mass of thin fibres

Chrysotile

Borax

Crystal is prismatic

Spheroidal adamite

Rounded, "spheroidal" crystal

Goethite

Soap contains boron derived from borax

Soap

Limonite groundmass is also a hydroxide mineral

Hydroxide minerals are typically "secondary minerals" that form when water reacts with existing rocks and minerals. Other mineral groups can become "hydrated", when water molecules are incorporated into the crystal structure.

Bauxite is a source of the metal aluminium, which is used to make everything from aircraft bodies to windows and kitchen foil and has an unusual texture. **Pisolitic bauxite** consists of grains and concretions of aluminium-rich minerals. **Diaspore** also contains aluminium,

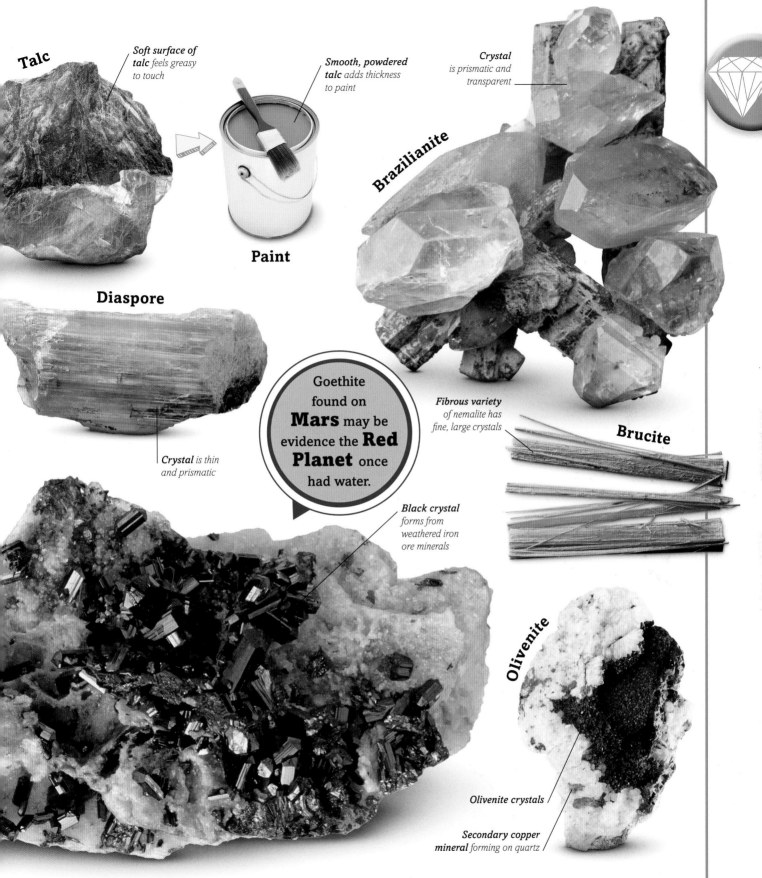

Talc

Soft surface of *talc* feels greasy to touch

Smooth, powdered *talc* adds thickness to paint

Paint

Crystal is prismatic and transparent

Brazilianite

Diaspore

Crystal is thin and prismatic

Goethite found on **Mars** may be evidence the **Red Planet** once had water.

Fibrous variety of nemalite has fine, large crystals

Brucite

Black crystal forms from weathered iron ore minerals

Olivenite

Olivenite crystals

Secondary copper mineral forming on quartz

but has long, thin crystals. **Borax** is used in household cleaning products and laundry **soap**, and is added to glass to make it heatproof. Flameproof asbestos used to be made from thin, hairlike crystal fibres of **chrysotile**, but its use in buildings is banned today because breathing in the tiny dust particles it creates causes fatal health problems. **Talc** is one of the softest known minerals. As well as talcum powder that keeps babies' bottoms rash-free, it is used as a filler to bulk out **paints**, plastics, and rubber, and is even added to some foods, such as bread.

Mineral salts

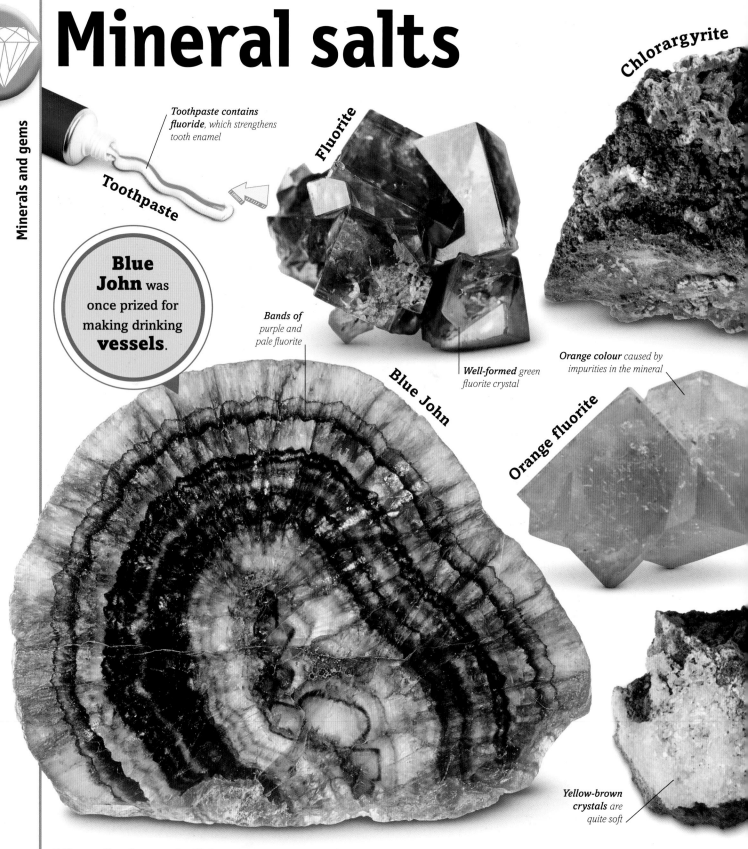

Chlorargyrite

*Toothpaste contains **fluoride**, which strengthens tooth enamel*

Fluorite

Toothpaste

Blue John was once prized for making drinking **vessels**.

Bands of purple and pale fluorite

Well-formed green fluorite crystal

Orange colour caused by impurities in the mineral

Blue John

Orange fluorite

Yellow-brown crystals are quite soft

Mineral salts, or halides, are a group of sometimes brightly coloured minerals that form when metals pair up with one of the halogen elements – fluorine, chlorine, bromine, or iodine. Many dissolve in water, so are left behind when saltwater evaporates.

Fluorite is calcium fluoride and comes in many strikingly beautiful colours – purple, orange, and green are the most common. **Blue John** is a stunning and rare purple-, yellow-, and white-banded fluorite. When metals are smelted, fluorite is used as a "flux" – a substance that

Carnallite

Mineral has a granular texture

Mineral turns purple when exposed to light

Halite

Cubic salt crystal on rocky groundmass

Calomel crystals

Toxic calomel is a mercury chloride

Striking royal-blue colour

Diaboleite

Sal ammoniac

Sylvite

Pink, grainy crystals of sylvite mixed with bands of quartz

Jarlite

Waxy masses of jarlite form as a crust

lowers the melting point of impurities, which makes them runnier and easier to separate from the metals. Other halides include the silver ore **chlorargyrite**, **sylvite** (used to make potassium fertilizer), and **sal ammoniac** (a rare aluminium chloride mineral used in the salty Nordic liquorice salmiakki). But by far the most common halide mineral, and one of the most important minerals on Earth, is rock salt, or **halite**. As well as being used to flavour and preserve food, it is spread on roads in winter to prevent ice forming and is also an important industrial chemical.

79

Salt

Salt crystals form as water in manmade pools evaporates

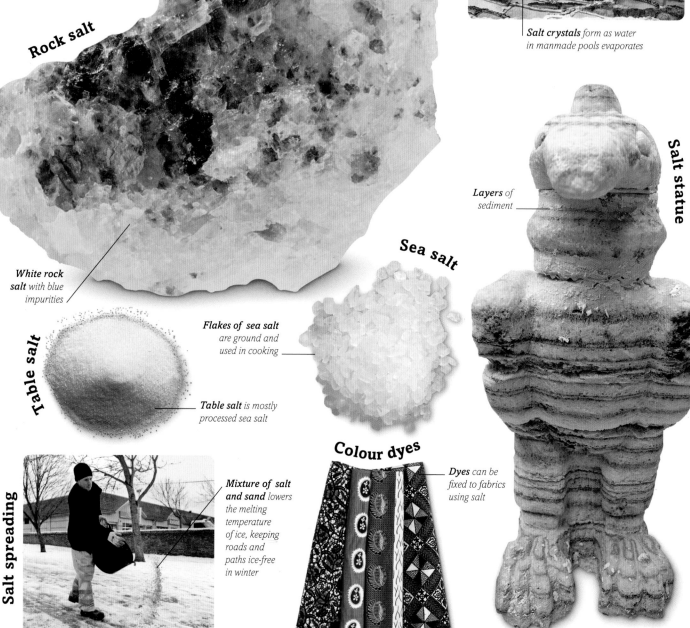

Cubic crystal of halite

Rock salt

White rock salt with blue impurities

Table salt

Table salt is mostly processed sea salt

Sea salt

Flakes of sea salt are ground and used in cooking

Colour dyes

Dyes can be fixed to fabrics using salt

Salt statue

Layers of sediment

Salt spreading

Mixture of salt and sand lowers the melting temperature of ice, keeping roads and paths ice-free in winter

Pure white crystals of salt are abundant on Earth. Essential for all animal life, salt can be extracted from rock deposits or salty waters. Salt is a halide mineral made of sodium chloride, which has been mined and traded since ancient times.

Rock salt, also known as **halite**, forms in vast deposits underground. The **Wieliczka Salt Mines**, in Poland, have been mined for a thousand years. Since most halides dissolve in water (they make seawater salty), deposits of these minerals occur in dry places where

Regular, cubic crystals

Up to **900 tonnes** of salt per hour can be extracted from large salt mines.

Halite

Salting removes water from cod and helps preserve it

Salted cod

Wieliczka Salt Mines Chapel, Poland

Church carved from solid salt 400 m (1,312 ft) underground

Salt is scraped into small mounds to evaporate the water

Salar de Uyuni, Bolivia

water evaporates. The **Salar de Uyuni**, in southwest Bolivia, is the world's largest salt flat. Evaporating salty water in shallow, manmade pools also pools produces salt. The **Maras Salt Mines** in Peru have produced salt for over 600 years. Salt is **spread on roads** in the winter to stop ice forming. It is also used to **preserve food**, as well as to flavour it. Small amounts of salt are an essential part of the diet, but if you consistently eat too much of it, it can cause health problems later in life.

Carbonates and borates

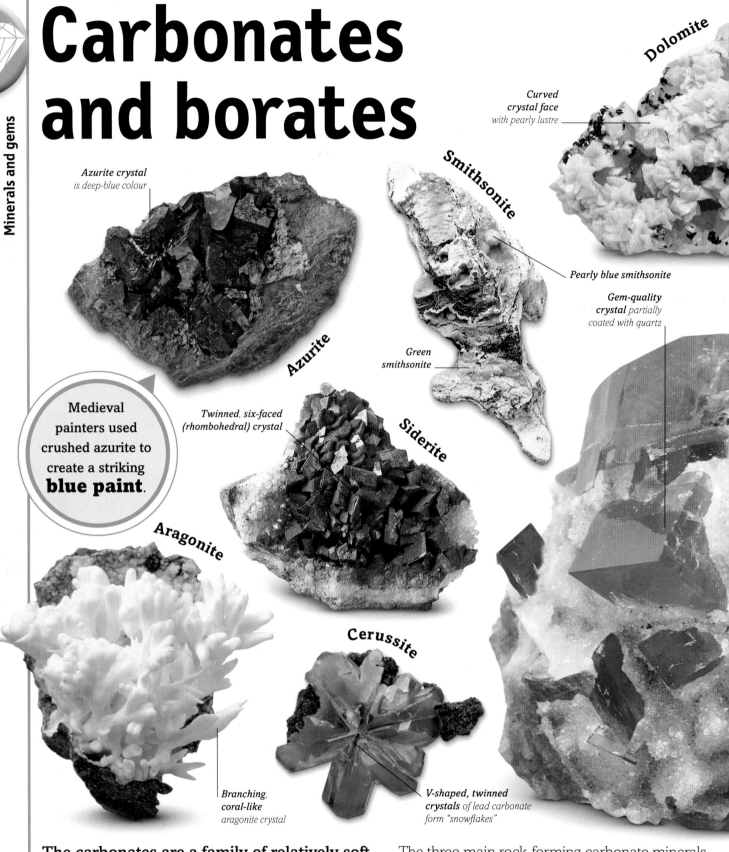

Dolomite
Curved crystal face *with pearly lustre*

Azurite crystal *is deep-blue colour*

Smithsonite
Pearly blue smithsonite

Azurite

Green smithsonite

Gem-quality **crystal** *partially coated with quartz*

Medieval painters used crushed azurite to create a striking **blue paint**.

Twinned, six-faced (rhombohedral) crystal

Siderite

Aragonite

Cerussite

Branching, coral-like *aragonite crystal*

V-shaped, twinned **crystals** *of lead carbonate form "snowflakes"*

The carbonates are a family of relatively soft minerals that are formed of metal elements, along with carbon and oxygen. Carbonates are abundant in sea water, and some sea creatures such as molluscs and snails are able to use carbonate minerals to build their shells.

The three main rock-forming carbonate minerals are **calcite**, **aragonite**, and **dolomite**. The most common is calcite – a calcium carbonate mineral. It has more than 1,000 shapes – more than any other mineral – including Iceland spar, which was once used to make lenses, and jagged **dogtooth**

Ankerite

Brown, six-faced (rhombohedral) crystal

Magnesite

Crystalline mass of magnesite on rock groundmass

Strontianite

Slender, needlelike crystals

Malachite

Rounded, kidney-shaped **masses** of tiny crystals called "botryoidal"

Pale yellowish brown crystal

Sinhalite

Rhodochrosite

Hambergite

Prismatic crystal

Crystals are white in pure form

Calcite – dogtooth spar

Parallel, needlelike crystals

Ulexite

COLOSSAL CALCITE

Biggest calcite crystal (280 tonnes)

School bus (Weight of 28 buses: 280 tonnes)

Monster mineral
Some calcite crystals are giants. The largest single crystal ever was found in Iceland. It weighed 280 tonnes, approximately the weight of 28 school buses.

spar. Carbonates can be a source of metals – **smithsonite** contains zinc and **magnesite** contains magnesium. **Rhodochrosite** is a manganese ore, the colour of which varies between rose pink to a deep crimson red, depending on how much **siderite** (iron carbonate) is mixed with it. Both **azurite** and **malachite** are weathered hydroxide minerals that often form together. Malachite is both a decorative stone and an important copper ore. Azurite is sometimes used in jewellery, but it is too soft to make a great gemstone, and loses its sparkle when heated.

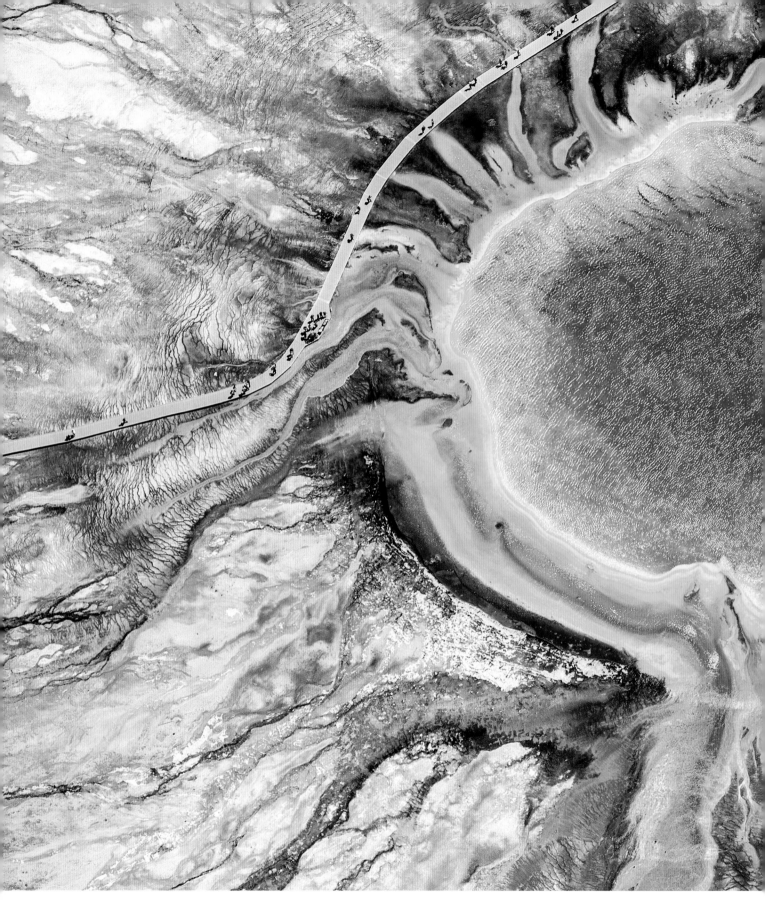

SPECTACULAR SPRING
Grand Prismatic Spring in Yellowstone National Park, USA, is the third largest hot spring in the world. It dazzles with colour: from deep blue at the centre, where the water is hottest, to orange and red at the edges, where it is cooler. This kaleidoscope of colours is caused by different types of bacteria living in each of the temperature zones and by the presence of certain minerals (such as sulfur).

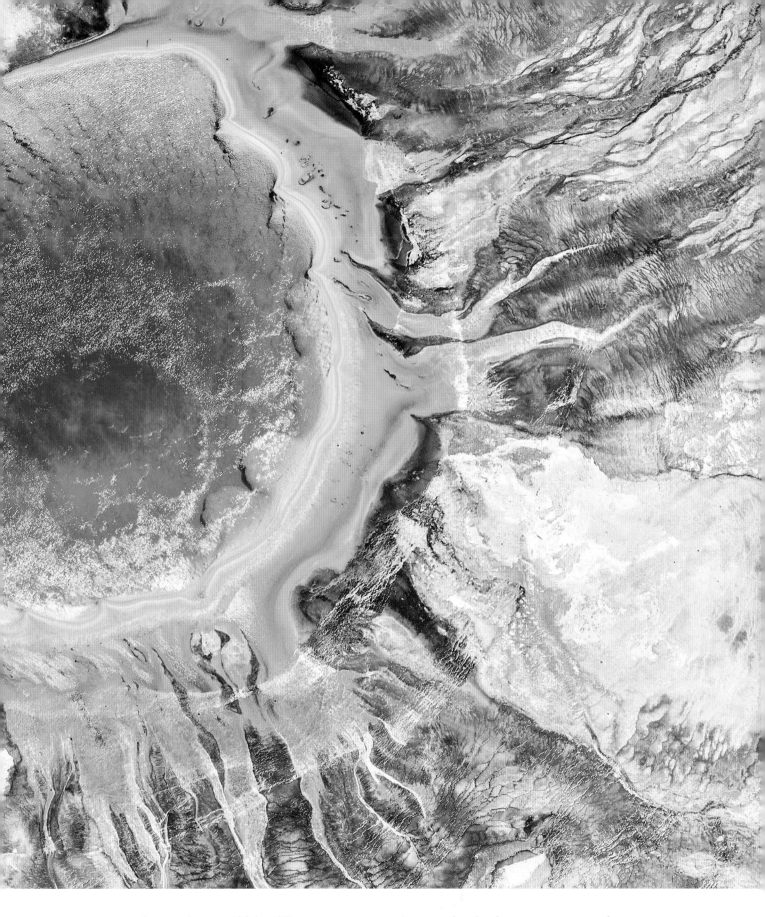

Water, with a temperature of up to 85°C (185°F), constantly wells up in the centre of the Grand Prismatic Spring. The energy to generate this hot water, and nearly 10,000 other springs, mudpots, and geysers in the area, comes from a supervolcano sitting below the park, which last erupted 640,000 years ago. The supervolcano's vast magma chamber heats water to more than 400°C (752°F) slowly transforming the rocks underneath as extremely hot fluids from the volcano dissolve the minerals contained in them. These fluids deposit new minerals in cavities and cracks, and cause minerals within the rock to change.

Malachite

Botryoidal malachite

Rounded lumps of malachite

Growth rings show how the mineral builds up in layers

Urn and base carved from malachite

Statue carved from malachite

Malachite statue

St Isaac's Cathedral, Russia

Column clad in carved malachite

Radiating crystals

Jewellery box

Jewellery box clad with thin veneers of malachite

Malachite urn

Bright green block with bands of darker colour

Stripy malachite

The name malachite comes from a Greek word meaning green, and it is easy to see why. This deep-green mineral is the natural form of copper carbonate hydroxide. It has been used for centuries as a source of copper and for making ornaments.

A green crust of malachite is a sign that other copper minerals are present below the surface, and prospectors look for this sign as they survey an area for valuable minerals. Malachite typically forms when copper ores react with acidic water containing carbonate. The larger specimens

Malachite pendant

Polished surface shows bands inside stone

Ancient Egyptian painting

Blue colour in this ancient wall painting comes from malachite pigment

Malachite

Some malachite **forms as stalactites** in cave formations.

Malachite stalactite

Group of radiating, fibrous crystals

Aztec knife

Wooden handle decorated with malachite chips

Azurite in malachite

Blue-coloured azurite is often mixed with malachite

Fibrous malachite

Malachite pigment

Blue-green powder is used in paints and make-up

form as **botryoidal** (grapelike) masses made up of lumps and bumps. Each bump contains many layers of crystals, so when the mineral is cut and polished it results in a rippled, flowerlike finish. Malachite is quite soft and is easily carved into **statues** and other ornaments.

About 16,000 kg (35,280 lb) of malachite is used to decorate various features at **St Isaac's Cathedral** in Russia. Powdered malachite mixed with water or oil was an early source of **pigments** and was used by artists in many ancient paintings.

Sulfate minerals

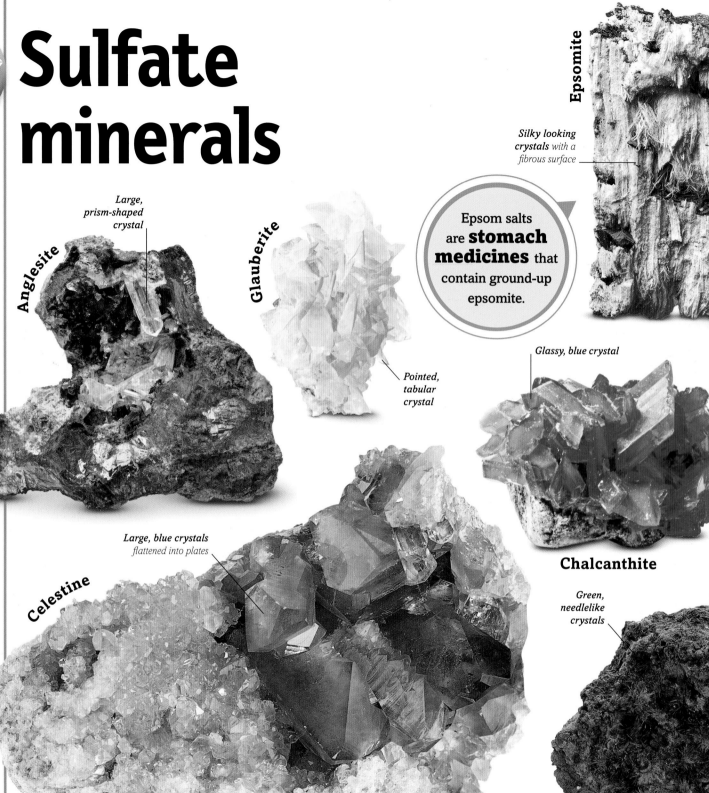

Anglesite

Large, prism-shaped crystal

Glauberite

Pointed, tabular crystal

Epsomite

Silky looking crystals with a fibrous surface

Epsom salts are **stomach medicines** that contain ground-up epsomite.

Glassy, blue crystal

Chalcanthite

Celestine

Large, blue crystals flattened into plates

Green, needlelike crystals

The sulfates, tungstates, chromates, and molybdates are minerals that show a similar chemical structure. Oxygen combines with sulfur, tungsten, chromium, and molybdenum respectively to form these minerals. The sulfates are the commonest.

Many of the sulfate minerals are important sources of useful metals. **Anglesite**, named after the Welsh island of Anglesey, is a lead sulfate. **Celestine** is a source of the metal strontium. Powdered strontium is added to fireworks to make red sparks when they explode. Celestine

Crocoite

Deep-red *crystal* with a greasy appearance

Scheelite

Tungsten filament made from scheelite

Light bulb

Cream-coloured, pyramid-shaped crystal

Flattened, glassy crystals form a spiky cluster

Baryte

Wulfenite

Gold-coloured crystals form overlapping plates

Brochantite

Blue, radiating, hairlike crystals

Cyanotrichite

Fibrous crystals

Gypsum

is also sought after for its beautiful, pale-coloured crystals. **Wulfenite** is purified into molybdenum, which is a metal used to make hard, armoured steel. Tungsten is refined from **scheelite** – named for the Swedish chemist Carl Scheele, who discovered the metal in 1781. Tungsten has the highest melting point of any metal and is used in heaters and light bulbs. In medicine, patients with intestine problems swallow "barium meals" (of which powdered **baryte** is an ingredient) so that their intestines show up on X-rays.

Gypsum

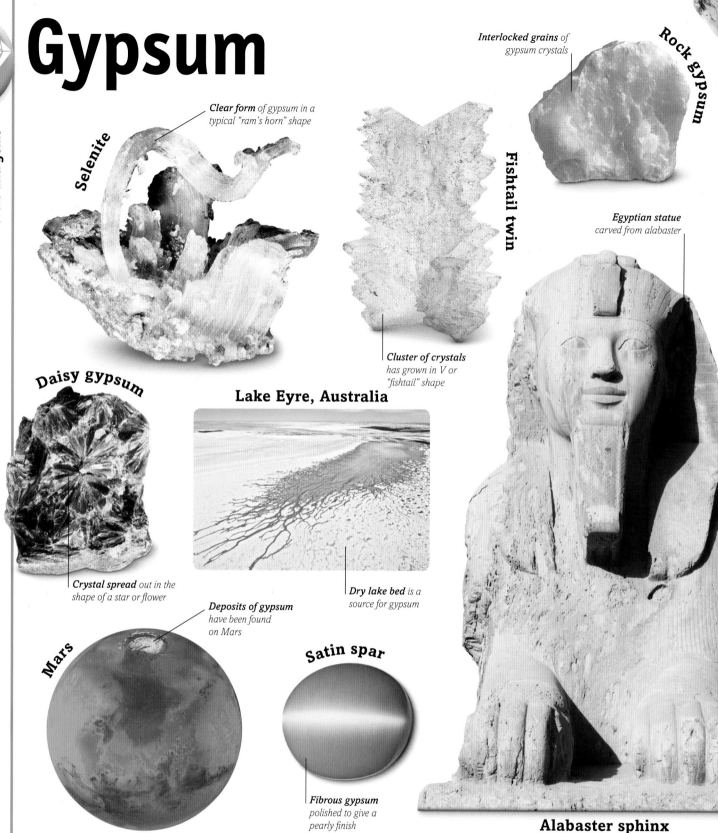

Selenite

Clear form of gypsum in a typical "ram's horn" shape

Fishtail twin

Cluster of crystals has grown in V or "fishtail" shape

Interlocked grains of gypsum crystals

Rock gypsum

Egyptian statue carved from alabaster

Daisy gypsum

Crystal spread out in the shape of a star or flower

Lake Eyre, Australia

Dry lake bed is a source for gypsum

Deposits of gypsum have been found on Mars

Mars

Satin spar

Fibrous gypsum polished to give a pearly finish

Alabaster sphinx

Gypsum is the natural form of calcium sulfate and is one of the world's most useful minerals – 200 million tonnes of it are dug up every year. Gypsum is used mostly to make the plasterboard or sheetrock that covers the inside walls of our homes.

Gypsum crystals form when water containing dissolved calcium and sulfate ions dries out. As a result, gypsum is common in desert areas, where lakes often dry out, and in deep caverns that were once filled with water. Large crystals of gypsum are called **selenite**, and they are mostly

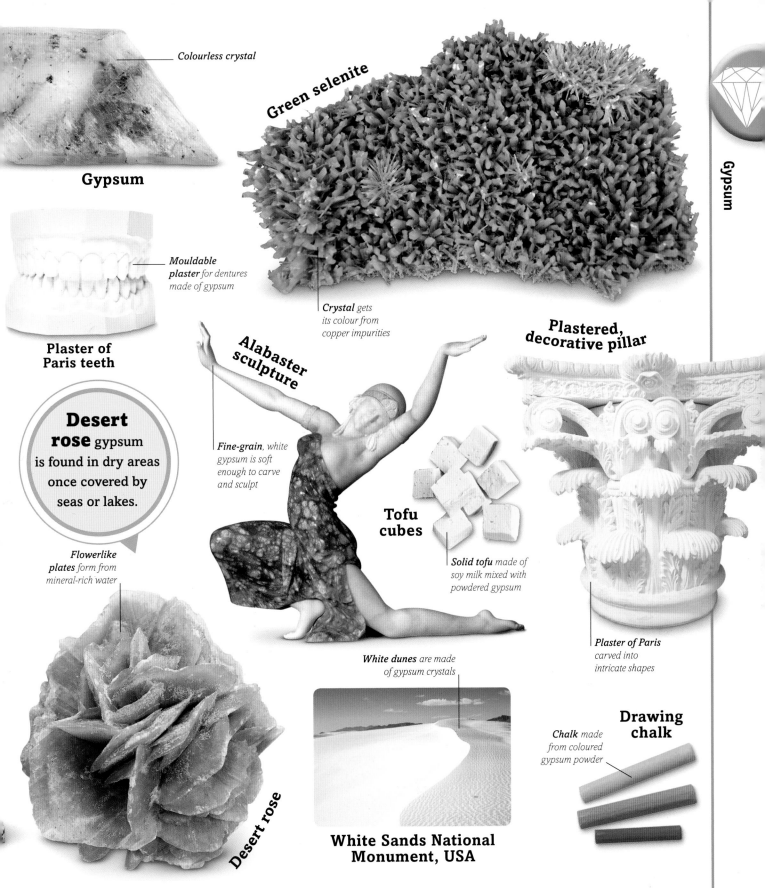

Colourless crystal

Gypsum

Green selenite

Mouldable plaster for dentures made of gypsum

Plaster of Paris teeth

Crystal gets its colour from copper impurities

Desert rose gypsum is found in dry areas once covered by seas or lakes.

Alabaster sculpture

Plastered, decorative pillar

Fine-grain, white gypsum is soft enough to carve and sculpt

Tofu cubes

Solid tofu made of soy milk mixed with powdered gypsum

Plaster of Paris carved into intricate shapes

Flowerlike plates form from mineral-rich water

White dunes are made of gypsum crystals

Drawing chalk

Chalk made from coloured gypsum powder

Desert rose

White Sands National Monument, USA

transparent and milk-coloured. Smaller crystals of gypsum make a white rock called gyprock, or **rock gypsum**. When the crystal grains are even finer, the mineral is known as **alabaster**, which is easy to carve and is used to make small statues and sculptures. Gypsum crystals have water trapped inside them. Heating the crystals drives out the water, making a dry powder called **plaster of Paris**. Adding water to plaster makes a paste that can be moulded and spread. As it dries, the water goes back into the crystals, making a hard, solid substance.

CAVE OF CRYSTALS

In 2000, some miners drilling more than 300 m (984 ft) below the surface in the Naica mines of northern Mexico made an incredible discovery. Breaking through a cave wall, they discovered a chamber never seen by human eyes. The *Cueva de los Cristales*, or Cave of Crystals, was filled floor to ceiling with monumental gypsum crystals that had grown undisturbed for millions of years.

The giant, translucent crystals in the cave are made of a type of gypsum called selenite. This is a commonplace mineral, but their sheer size makes the crystals a wonder of nature. Some of them are more than 10 m (33 ft) long. For millions of years, these caves were flooded with groundwater rich in calcium sulfate. Kept warm by heat from a magma chamber below, the colossal pillars of selenite crystals grew steadily. When the mines were drained of water the crystals were revealed. However, once the mines are exhausted and the water pumps are turned off, the cave will be flooded once again. For now, 100 per cent humidity and temperatures reaching 50°C (122°F) keep this natural wonder stable.

Phosphate group minerals

Turquoise

Encrusted turquoise

Iron oxide groundmass

Crystals are elongated and prismatic

Vivianite

Fine crystal of light blue-green phosphophyllite

Variscite

Hard, compact mass of variscite in a rock that has been split open to show its waxy lustre

Apatite

Well-formed prismatic crystal

Blue ochre

Powdered vivianite makes a deep-blue pigment

Pyromorphite

Typical, barrel-shaped crystals

Variscite was named after the German district **Variscia**, where it was discovered.

The phosphates are a family of minerals that contain phosphorus and oxygen. They are part of a large and varied group that includes the arsenates and vanadates. Bright colours are characteristic of this group of minerals.

Turquoise has been mined for thousands of years and was a very important mineral for many ancient cultures. Semiprecious **variscite** is often mistaken for turquoise, but is greener. **Vivianite** turns pale blue to a dark greenish-blue when exposed to light. **Apatite** is

Phosphophyllite

Wavellite grows as circular plates of radiating crystals

Wavellite

Yellow crust of powdery carnotite on sandstone

Carnotite

Match heads contain phosphorus, which comes from wavellite

Matchsticks

Radiating crystal forms a rosette

Clinoclase

Adamantine (glossy), prismatic crystal

Mimetite

Mimetite crystals resemble those of pyromorphite

Striking purple crystals contain cobalt and arsenic

Erythrite

Spanner

Spanner contains vanadium (of which vanadinite is a major source), chromium, and other metals alloyed with steel

Vanadinite

the most common phosphate mineral. In the body, it builds our teeth enamel and bones. In rocks, it occurs as a group of related minerals including chlorapatite and fluorapatite. The main use of phosphate minerals is as fertilizer – 200,000 tonnes of phosphate-containing rocks are crushed every year to make fertilizer. The phosphate family includes vanadates (with vanadium) and arsenates (with arsenic). Cobalt-containing **erythrite** is an arsenate. The vanadate **carnotite** is an important source of radioactive uranium, used to generate nuclear power.

Silicates

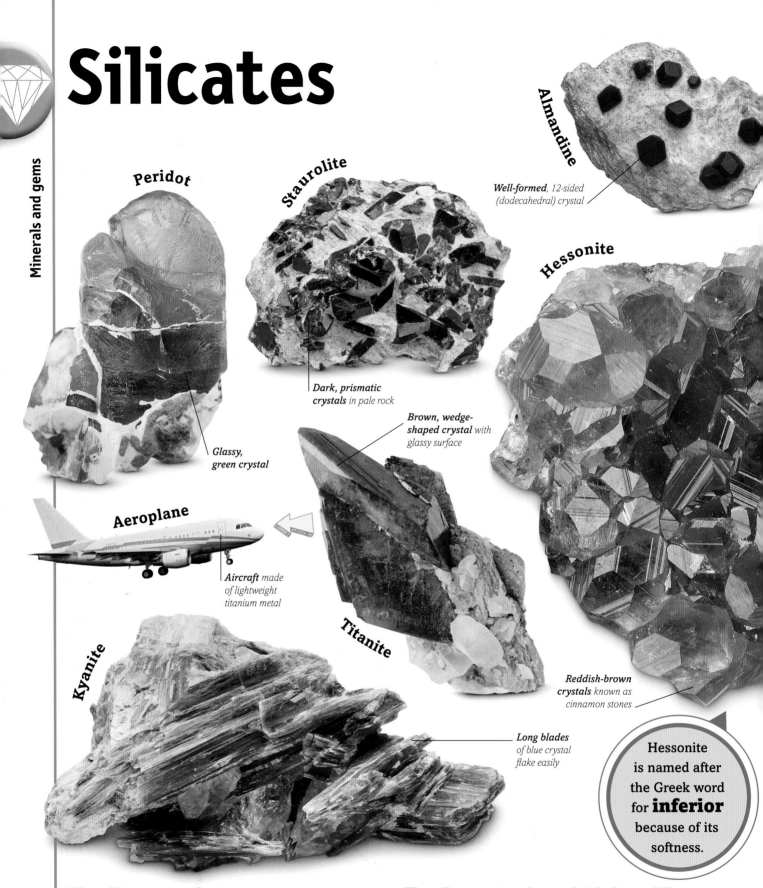

Almandine

Well-formed, 12-sided (dodecahedral) crystal

Peridot

Staurolite

Glassy, green crystal

Dark, prismatic crystals in pale rock

Hessonite

Brown, wedge-shaped crystal with glassy surface

Aeroplane

Aircraft made of lightweight titanium metal

Titanite

Kyanite

Long blades of blue crystal flake easily

Reddish-brown crystals known as cinnamon stones

Hessonite is named after the Greek word for **inferior** because of its softness.

The silicates are the most common minerals on Earth. They are made up of silicon and oxygen, combined with other elements, mostly metals. These minerals are the main ingredients in sands and clays, and are found in almost all rocks.

The silicate minerals are divided into different groups based on their structure. The ones seen here are nesosilicates or sorosilicates. **Peridot** belongs to a subgroup of nesosilicates called olivine. It is one of the major minerals that make up Earth's upper mantle. **Almandine** and

Uvarovite

Necklace set with colourless zircons

Large, brown crystal

Zircon

Zircon necklace

Crust of green crystals contains chromium

Epidote

Shiny, greenish crystals form prism shapes with ridges

Vesuvianite

Tanzanite

Yellow-green crystals have striped ridges called striations

Glassy, blue crystal is sometimes mistaken for sapphire

Large, prismatic crystal growing out of feldspar

Hemimorphite

Topaz

Rounded, grape-shaped lumps made of tiny crystals

hessonite are members of the garnet group of nesosilicates. These minerals are harder than most minerals, but are softer than the gem minerals corundum, diamond, beryl, and topaz, which is why they were used in jewellery in ancient times. The nesosilicates **staurolite** and **kyanite** are valuable sources of the metal aluminium. **Vesuvianite**, a sorosilicate, is named after Mount Vesuvius in Italy, where it was first discovered. **Epidote** is another sorosilicate, but is only rarely used as a gem material.

Rhodonite

Rose-coloured crystals form brittle plates

Rhodonite can be carved into many shapes, such as this box

Carved rhodonite box

Wollastonite

Fibrous layers of crystals splinter easily

Golden crystals crack into leafy flakes

Astrophyllite

Dark crystal is nearly opaque

Augite

Black tourmaline

Indicolite

Large, blue crystal

Dark, prismatic crystal

SUPER GROUP

Other minerals

Silicates

Minerals in Earth's crust

Widespread silicates
There are about 1,000 kinds of silicate. They make up 90 per cent of the minerals in Earth's rocky crust and mantle.

Inosilicate minerals take their name from the Greek word for "thread", because of the chainlike structure of the crystals. They include **augite**, which is one of the most common minerals in basalt and other dark-coloured igneous rocks. **Wollastonite** forms when limestone is heated by magma underground. **Rhodonite** gets its name from the Greek word for rose. Its pink colour comes from manganese in its crystal structure. A common inosilicate called **hornblende** was often mistaken for a valuable ore mineral. The cyclosilicate minerals

Beryl: morganite

Pink crystals

Long, six-sided
(hexagonal) crystal

Beryl: heliodor

The
largest
mineral **crystal**
is a beryl
**18 m (59 ft)
long**.

Hornblende

Green-blue,
*prism-shaped crystals
form a sparkly crust*

Dark crystals grow
in long prisms with
striations on side

Watermelon tourmaline

Red crystal surrounded
by green tourmaline

Dioptase

*Pink crystal
has curved faces*

Elbaite

have crystal structures made up of rings of silicate groups. Tourmaline is one of the most common cyclosilicates and comes in many colour varieties, most of which are used as gems. The most abundant type is **black tourmaline**. Another colourful cyclosilicate is

beryl. **Morganite** is its pink form, while **heliodor** is a yellow variety. Vivid green beryl is more famous and it is called emerald. **Dioptase** is sometimes mistaken for emerald, but its crystals are much more fragile and break too easily to use in jewellery.

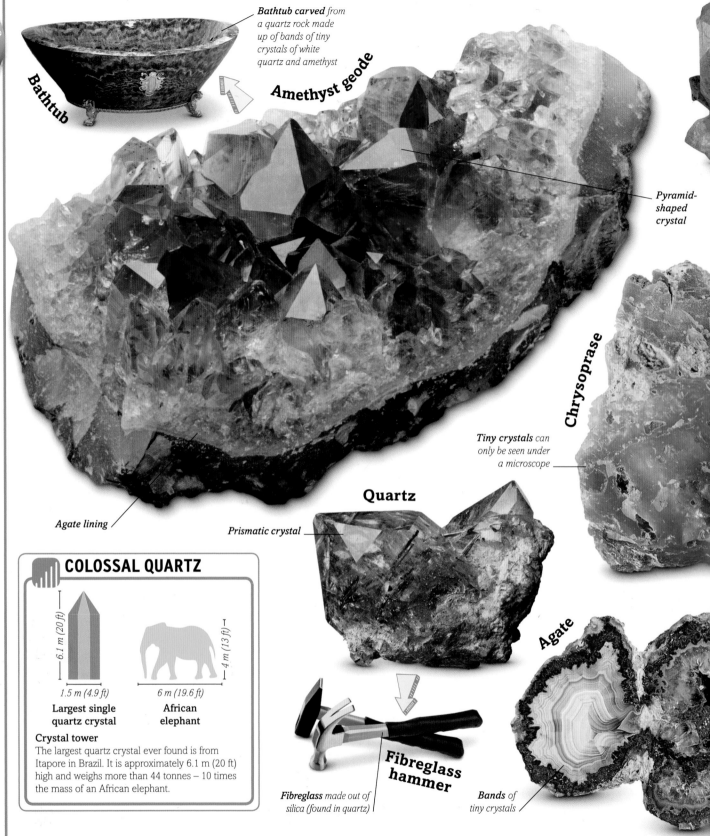

Bathtub carved from a quartz rock made up of bands of tiny crystals of white quartz and amethyst

Bathtub

Amethyst geode

Chrysoprase

Pyramid-shaped crystal

Tiny crystals can only be seen under a microscope

Quartz

Agate lining

Prismatic crystal

Agate

COLOSSAL QUARTZ

6.1 m (20 ft)

4 m (13 ft)

1.5 m (4.9 ft)
Largest single quartz crystal

6 m (19.6 ft)
African elephant

Crystal tower
The largest quartz crystal ever found is from Itapore in Brazil. It is approximately 6.1 m (20 ft) high and weighs more than 44 tonnes – 10 times the mass of an African elephant.

Fibreglass hammer

Fibreglass made out of silica (found in quartz)

Bands of tiny crystals

Quartz is one of the most common minerals on the surface of Earth. Sand is made up mostly of grains of quartz crystals, and the mineral is found in common rocks, such as granite and sandstone. Quartz is the main example of a tectosilicate, a type of silicate in which the crystal structure consists of a spiral-like arrangement of silicate groups. There are many colour varieties of quartz. **Amethyst** is purple quartz and gets its colour from iron impurities. It is named after the maiden Amethyst from Greek mythology. Many amethysts and similar kinds of

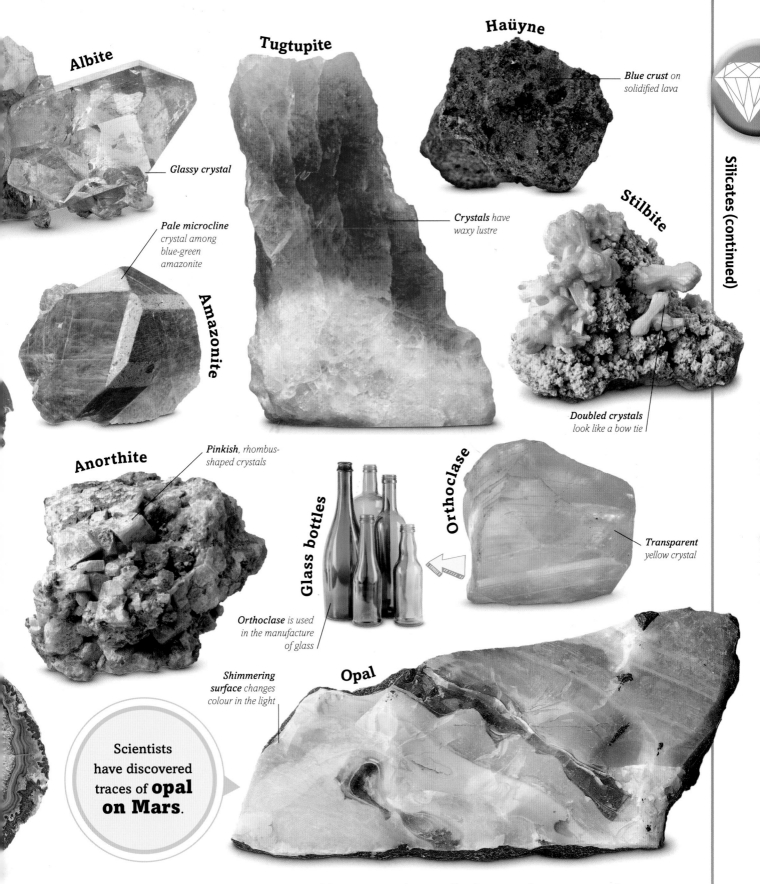

Albite

Glassy crystal

Tugtupite

Haüyne

Blue crust on solidified lava

Pale microcline crystal among blue-green amazonite

Amazonite

Crystals have waxy lustre

Stilbite

Anorthite

Pinkish, rhombus-shaped crystals

Glass bottles

Orthoclase

Orthoclase is used in the manufacture of glass

Doubled crystals look like a bow tie

Transparent yellow crystal

Shimmering surface changes colour in the light

Opal

Scientists have discovered traces of **opal on Mars**.

crystalline quartz form as geodes – air bubbles inside rocks that become filled with mineral-rich water from which crystals slowly form. **Agate** is a microcrystalline, meaning the crystals are tiny, giving the mineral a smooth texture. **Opal** is made up of silica and water, and typically does not have a crystal structure. **Albite** and **orthoclase** are examples of feldspars, which are the main silicates in rocks. **Stilbite** crystals are tabular in shape, have a pearly lustre, and can exceed 10 cm (4 in) in length.

Topaz

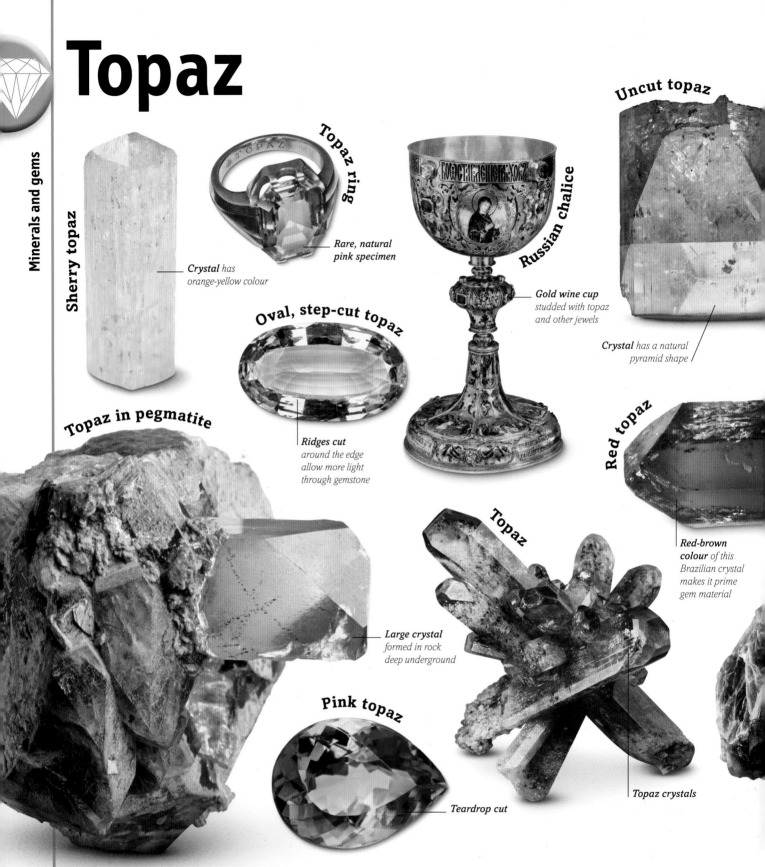

Sherry topaz

Crystal *has orange-yellow colour*

Topaz ring

Rare, natural *pink specimen*

Uncut topaz

Crystal *has a natural pyramid shape*

Russian chalice

Gold wine cup *studded with topaz and other jewels*

Oval, step-cut topaz

Ridges cut *around the edge allow more light through gemstone*

Red topaz

Red-brown colour *of this Brazilian crystal makes it prime gem material*

Topaz in pegmatite

Large crystal *formed in rock deep underground*

Topaz

Topaz crystals

Pink topaz

Teardrop cut

The word topaz comes from Sanskrit, an ancient Indian language, and means "fire" – a reference to its golden-yellow colour. In the past, many yellowish gems, such as peridot and garnets, were called topaz. The gem was used in ancient Egypt, Greece, and Rome.

The earliest source of topaz was an island in the Red Sea called Zabargad, which was known as Topazios in ancient times. However, it is thought the gems found there were actually peridot. In Sri Lanka, topaz crystals are found among the pebbles of river beds, where the gems have been rounded

Topaz necklace

*Small, blue topaz **stone** polished to give it a curved surface*

Golden brown variety is called sherry topaz

Sherry topaz

Cut shows off colour and shine

Mixed-cut topaz

Topaz in gold

Natural blue topaz can be very pale

Orange sections made of topaz

Topaz inlay in marble

Bluish-grey specimen

Statue wearing blue topaz

Blue topaz

Topaz on muscovite

MEGA CRYSTAL

17.53 cm (6.9 in)

American Golden Topaz

Topaz king
Dug up in the Minas Gerais area of Brazil, the American Golden Topaz is one of the largest cut yellow topaz crystals in the world. It is a 172-faceted gem weighing 4.58 kg (10 lb).

as a result of being knocked together by water currents. In other parts of the world, topaz has formed inside igneous rocks that have cooled slowly underground. Topaz occurs in granite, rhyolite, and **pegmatite** cavities. Most topaz specimens are yellow and brown. Colourless or grey stones are also common, while **pink** and blue ones are rarer. Orange-yellow, **sherry** stones from Brazil are particularly valuable. As well as its typical use in **necklaces** and **rings**, topaz is also used in **marble inlays** or other decorative objects, such as the **Russian chalice** shown above.

Jade

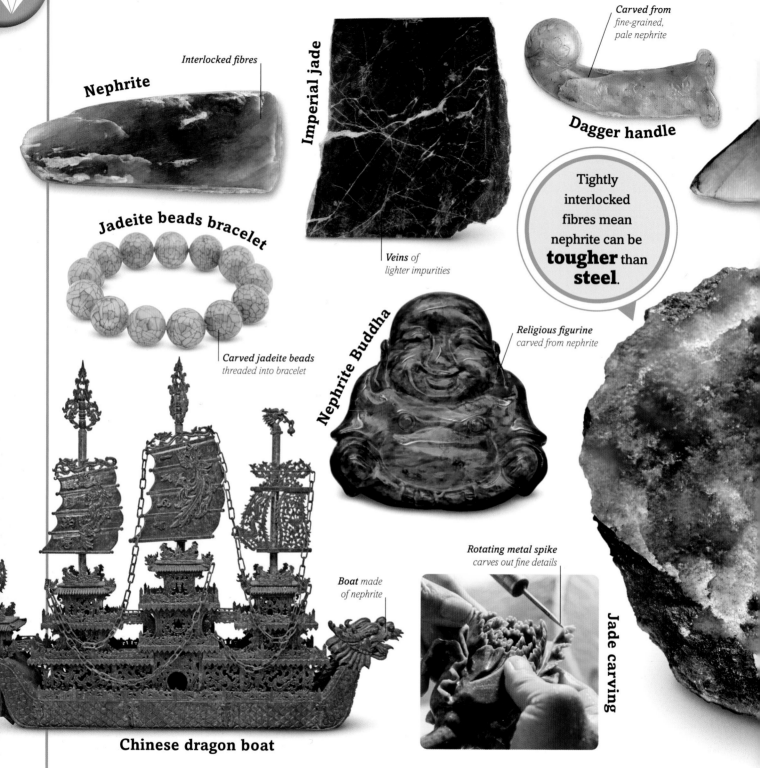

Nephrite

Interlocked fibres

Imperial jade

Veins of lighter impurities

Carved from fine-grained, pale nephrite

Dagger handle

Tightly interlocked fibres mean nephrite can be **tougher** than **steel**.

Jadeite beads bracelet

Carved jadeite beads threaded into bracelet

Nephrite Buddha

Religious figurine carved from nephrite

Boat made of nephrite

Rotating metal spike carves out fine details

Jade carving

Chinese dragon boat

Jade is a mostly green stone made of tiny crystals. It is very hard, but can be carved and polished into beautiful, smooth ornaments. Cultures all over the world have used it for many centuries to make jewellery.

Jade is not a single mineral, but a group of many. Green serpentine objects are often mistaken for jade. True jades are either **jadeite** or **nephrite**. Jadeite is an inosilicate containing sodium, aluminium, and iron, and occurs in fine crystals that interlock to form a waxy-looking

Lavender colour due to manganese impurities

Lavender jadeite

Mask carved out of jadeite

Mexican mask

GIANT JADE BUDDHA

Body carved from Canadian jade

2.7 m (8.8 ft) high

Base is made of alabaster

Jade Buddha for Universal Peace
Carved from a single piece of nephrite, this 4-tonne statue of the Buddha is based in Australia but is taken around the world for Buddhists to see.

Princess Tou Wan burial suit

Raw specimen of nephrite

Nephrite in groundmass

Yellow jade

Yellow jade is rare

Hundreds of jade **plates** sewn together with gold threads

Lilac jade

Chinese dragon vase

Carving makes use of the range of colours in the jadeite specimen

Weathered rind forms surface of jadeite cobble

mass. In its pure form, jadeite is creamy white, but impurities give most specimens their colour. Green comes from iron, **lilac** from manganese, and **yellow** forms have a range of extra elements. In ancient China, jade was believed to protect the dead from demons and ensure immortality, and extraordinary jade **burial suits** were created for kings and queens. Older Chinese jade objects are mostly made from nephrite, but more recent objects are made of jadeite, after the discovery of the mineral in Burma.

JASPER FALLS
In the southern Venezuelan state of Bolívar, in Canaima National Park, water flows over a red and black, tiger-striped river bed. Known as Kako Parú in the language of the indigenous Pemón people, these small cascades ripple and splash over solid jasper. The dappled sunlight shining through the jungle foliage sparkles on the semiprecious stone, creating a stunningly beautiful wonder of nature.

Some of the oldest sandstones in the world are found in the Guiana Shield, a vast block of rock that forms highlands in the northern parts of South America, dotted with strange table mountains called *tepuis*. Contained in these 2-billion-year-old rocks are younger minerals deposited by mineral-rich fluids in cracks and fissures. Jasper is a cryptocrystalline form of quartz – its crystals are intergrown and can only be seen with a microscope. Its red colour comes from iron impurities, while darker bands contain more iron. The way the tiny crystals absorb and reflect light gives the surface a waxy sheen and a shimmery depth. When the angle of the light is just right, the jasper stream bed glows golden.

Ruby and sapphire

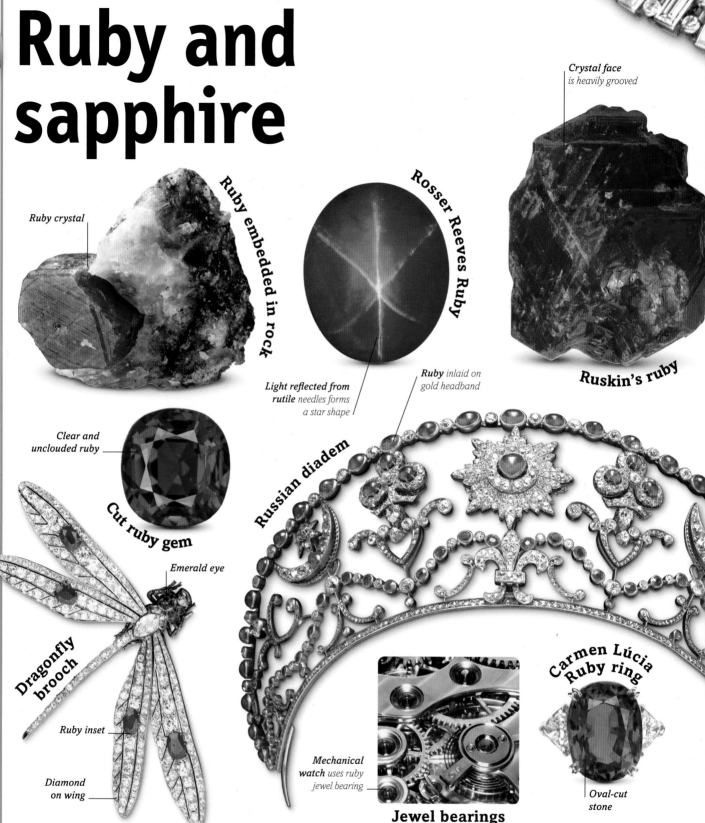

Ruby crystal

Ruby embedded in rock

Rosser Reeves Ruby

Light reflected from rutile needles forms a star shape

Crystal face is heavily grooved

Ruskin's ruby

Ruby inlaid on gold headband

Clear and unclouded ruby

Cut ruby gem

Russian diadem

Emerald eye

Dragonfly brooch

Ruby inset

Diamond on wing

Mechanical watch uses ruby jewel bearing

Jewel bearings

Carmen Lúcia Ruby ring

Oval-cut stone

Rubies are red, sapphires are blue, but both are the made of the same mineral – corundum. Impurities give these aluminium oxide minerals their colours. Rubies tend to be small (stones more than 10 carats are rare), while sapphires can grow large.

Rubies are gorgeous red stones found in marbles and metamorphosed limestones. The majority of gem-quality rubies, including the **Carmen Lúcia Ruby**, come from Myanmar. Chromium impurities give ruby its red colour. Symmetrically arranged, titanium-containing

Bismarck Sapphire pendant

Massive blue sapphire, surrounded by eight, smaller, square-cut sapphires and 312 diamonds

A sapphire can only be scratched by a **diamond** or another sapphire.

Sapphire gravels

Uncut sapphire gravel

Diamonds surrounding a 733-carat (146.6 g/ 5.1 oz) sapphire

Black Star of Queensland

Blue sapphire

Deep-blue, rough corundum

Rough sapphire *worn by water*

Uncut sapphire

Corundum

Crystal is six-sided

Pink sapphire

Logan Sapphire

Sapphire has been cut to have triangular faces

Synthetic corundum

Synthetic gemstone has no flaws of inclusions

Blue sapphire is 423-carat (84.6 g/2.9 oz)

needles of rutile grow inside rubies, such as in the beautiful **Rosser Reeves Ruby**. While rubies are only ever red, sapphires can be many colours. The most common colour is **blue**, while **pink sapphires** are also found. The 733-carat (146.6 g/5.1 oz) **Black Star of Queensland** is rare because of its size. Sapphires and rubies can also be produced artificially in laboratories. Today, the **jewel bearings** used to keep mechanical watches running smoothly are made of synthetic corundum.

Emerald

Emerald and diamond tiara

Aquamarine

Impurities give the hexagonal (six-sided) prism a blue-green colour

Emerald in rock

Emerald crystal in pegmatite

Cut emerald

Rectangular cut makes the gemstone sparkle

Emerald crystal

Turban ornament

Smooth, polished emerald set in gold

Hexagonal (six-sided) crystal

Emerald from Carniaba mine, Brazil

Crystal has the same structure and colour as natural emerald

Synthetic emerald

Emerald is one of the most valued gemstones, famed for its deep-green colour. It is often cut into a rectangle or square shape with angled edges. Emeralds form within thin veins of white calcite or quartz, in dark shale, and limestone.

Emerald is a variety of a mineral called beryl. Beryl is a silicate mineral that contains aluminium and beryllium. The word beryl means "pale" and pure specimens are see-through. A blue-green version is called **aquamarine**. Emerald, which gets its green colouring from tiny amounts of

Emerald crystal

Emerald in limestone matrix

Pear-shaped emerald on a tiara

Spanish Inquisition necklace

Barrel-shaped emerald weighs about 45 carats (9 g / 0.3 oz)

Emeralds were a symbol of fertility and life in ancient Egypt.

Emerald

Trapiche emerald

Sooty material trapped in the emerald forms a star shape

Cloudy, translucent emerald

Polished emerald

Large emerald embedded in quartz crystals

Prismatic emerald crystal

Crystal has a weathered appearance

Large emerald crystal with flat ends

Chalk emerald ring

Turkish dagger

Square-cut emerald set among diamond chips

Colombian emeralds on a ceremonial dagger

AWESOME EMERALD

5 cm (2 in)

Duke of Devonshire Emerald

Glittering gift
Given as a gift by the emperor of Brazil to the English Duke of Devonshire in 1831, this emerald is one of the largest ever found. The stone is 5 cm (2 in) long and weighs 277 g (8 oz).

chromium or vanadium impurities in the crystals is the most valued form of beryl. Emeralds have been highly prized since they were first mined in Egypt in 1300 BCE. Egypt was the main site for mining emeralds for a thousand years. Later, the finest specimens, including the **Chalk emerald** and the emeralds set in the **Spanish Inquisition necklace**, came from Colombian mines in the 18th and 19th centuries. **Synthetic** emeralds are formed from hot water filled with dissolved minerals that are allowed to crystallize slowly, but they are not considered to be minerals.

Feldspars

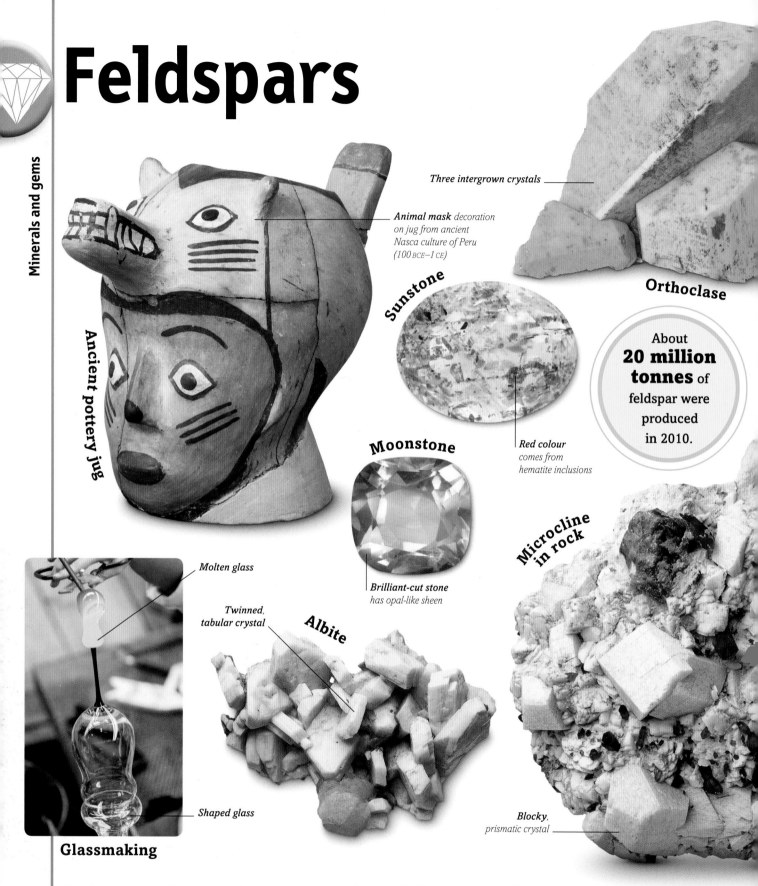

Three intergrown crystals

Animal mask decoration on jug from ancient Nasca culture of Peru *(100 BCE–1 CE)*

Orthoclase

Sunstone

Red colour comes from hematite inclusions

About **20 million tonnes** of feldspar were produced in 2010.

Ancient pottery jug

Moonstone

Brilliant-cut stone has opal-like sheen

Microcline in rock

Molten glass

Twinned, tabular crystal

Albite

Shaped glass

Blocky, prismatic crystal

Glassmaking

Feldspars are the most abundant minerals in Earth's crust. These aluminosilicates (silicates with aluminium) also make up the major part of igneous rocks. Beyond Earth, feldspars are also the most abundant minerals on the surface of the Moon.

Feldspars are not flashy minerals. They are almost never found in bright colours, and are generally seen in dull browns and tans. But this group of minerals play a crucial role in forming rocks. They fall into two groups – the alkali feldspars and the plagioclase feldspars. Minerals in both groups have

Persian ceramic water container

Water container
made of ceramic

Cleaning products

Cleaning powder
contains crushed feldspar

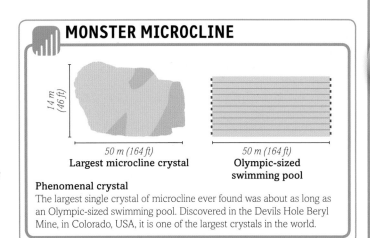

14 m (46 ft)

50 m (164 ft)
Largest microcline crystal

50 m (164 ft)
Olympic-sized swimming pool

Phenomenal crystal
The largest single crystal of microcline ever found was about as long as an Olympic-sized swimming pool. Discovered in the Devils Hole Beryl Mine, in Colorado, USA, it is one of the largest crystals in the world.

Amazonite

Blue-green microcline, or amazonite

Colour play on shimmery surface is called "schiller"

Labradorite

Well-formed crystal of sanidine

Sanidine

Andesine

Rare, red, gem-quality andesine

Pink granite coast, Brittany, France

Large, well-developed plagioclase feldspars form in granite rocks

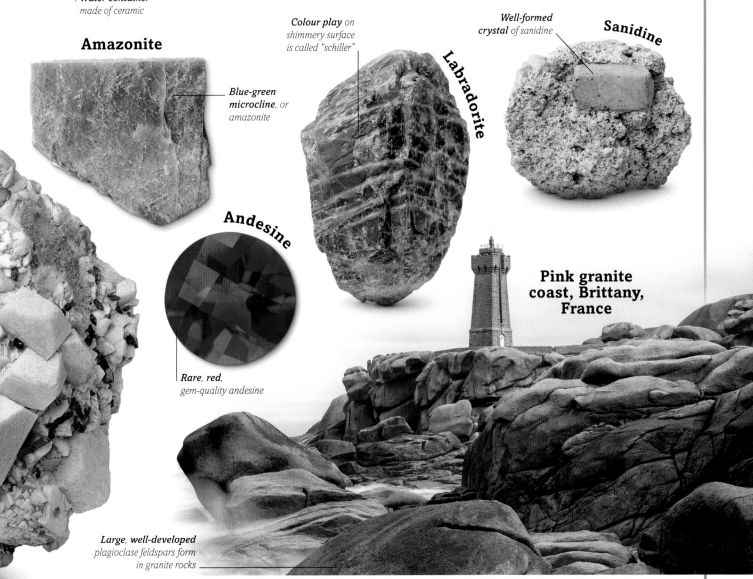

the same crystal structure, but their chemical composition varies. Alkali feldspars include potassium-rich **orthoclase**, **microcline**, and **sanidine**. **Andesine** contains a high percentage of calcium and sodium, while **labradorite** is considered a semiprecious plagioclase. Intergrown, tiny feldspar crystals make **moonstone**, which comes in blues and whites. Feldspars are used in **glassmaking** and **ceramics**, where they help to lower the melting temperature of a mixture. They are also crushed and used in **cleaning products**, and ground to make concrete.

Mineraloids

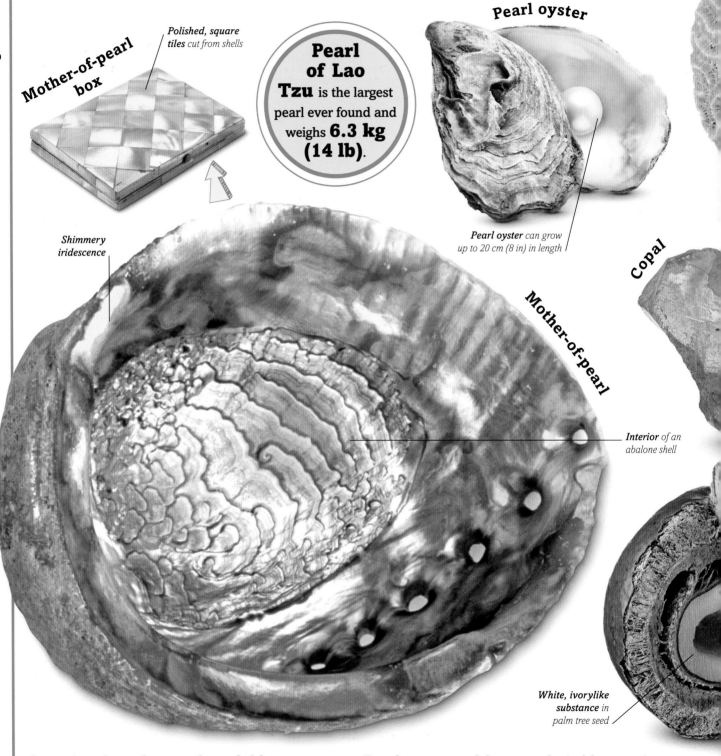

Mother-of-pearl box

Polished, square *tiles cut from shells*

Pearl of Lao Tzu is the largest pearl ever found and weighs **6.3 kg (14 lb)**.

Pearl oyster

Pearl oyster can grow up to 20 cm (8 in) in length

Copal

Mother-of-pearl

Shimmery iridescence

Interior of an abalone shell

White, ivorylike substance in palm tree seed

Organic minerals, or mineraloids, are often hard substances made by living things. Unlike minerals that have an ordered internal crystal arrangement, mineraloids may or may not have a regular crystal structure.

Pearls are one of the most desirable organic minerals. Made inside the shells of molluscs, they grow in layers around a small piece of grit or foreign particle. Some of the most beautiful **mother-of-pearl** comes from the abalone shell, with its silvery layers and

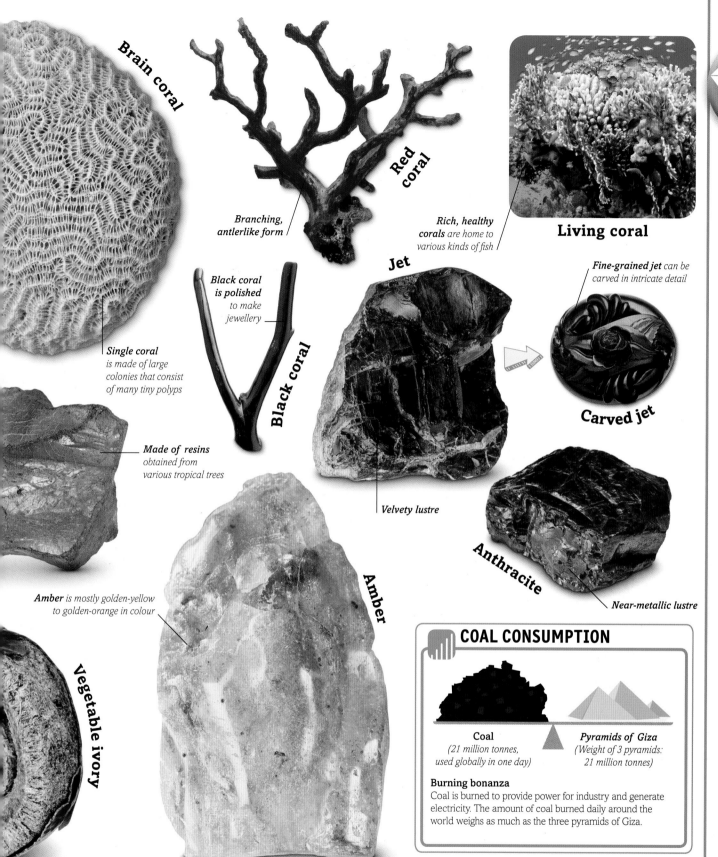

Brain coral

Red coral

Branching, antlerlike form

Rich, healthy corals are home to various kinds of fish

Living coral

Jet

Fine-grained jet can be carved in intricate detail

Black coral is polished to make jewellery

Black coral

Carved jet

Single coral is made of large colonies that consist of many tiny polyps

Made of resins obtained from various tropical trees

Velvety lustre

Anthracite

Near-metallic lustre

Amber is mostly golden-yellow to golden-orange in colour

Amber

Vegetable ivory

COAL CONSUMPTION

Coal
(21 million tonnes, used globally in one day)

Pyramids of Giza
(Weight of 3 pyramids: 21 million tonnes)

Burning bonanza
Coal is burned to provide power for industry and generate electricity. The amount of coal burned daily around the world weighs as much as the three pyramids of Giza.

iridescent, multi-coloured interior. As well as jewellery, mother-of-pearl from giant oysters is used for human bone implants. **Coral** is another hard structure made by living things. Tiny animals, called polyps, secrete a hard calcium carbonate skeleton to live in. Tough and compact, complex carvings can be made out of **red** and **black** coral. **Jet** and **anthracite** are forms of coal that are burned as fuel, but which can also be carved and polished. **Vegetable ivory**, from certain palm trees, is used in carvings and to make jewellery.

Amber

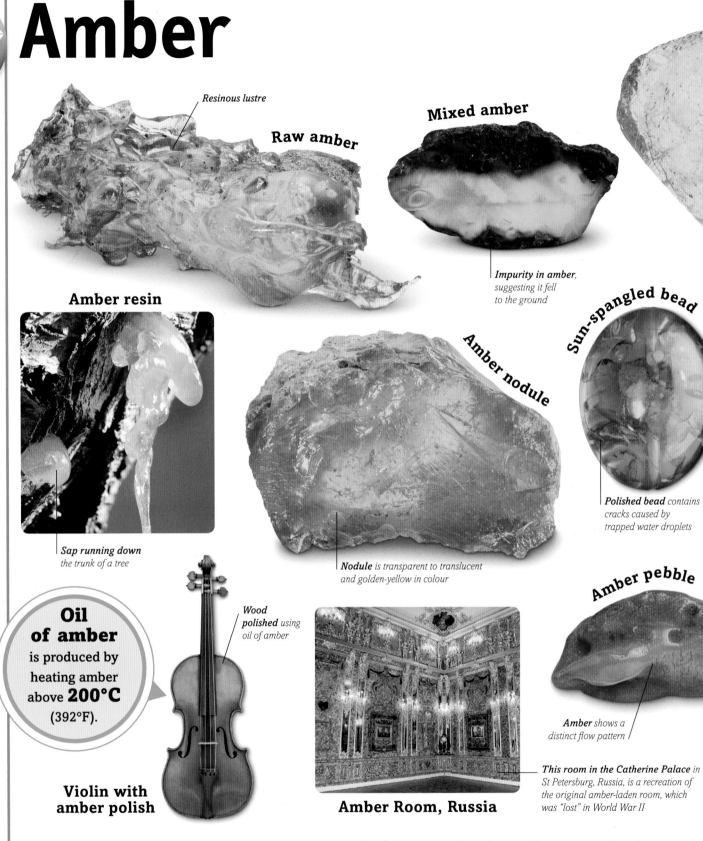

Resinous lustre

Raw amber

Mixed amber

Impurity in amber,
suggesting it fell
to the ground

Amber resin

Sap running down
the trunk of a tree

Amber nodule

Nodule is transparent to translucent
and golden-yellow in colour

Sun-spangled bead

Polished bead contains
cracks caused by
trapped water droplets

**Oil
of amber**
is produced by
heating amber
above **200°C**
(392°F).

Wood
polished *using*
oil of amber

**Violin with
amber polish**

Amber Room, Russia

This room in the Catherine Palace in
St Petersburg, Russia, is a recreation of
the original amber-laden room, which
was "lost" in World War II

Amber pebble

Amber shows a
distinct flow pattern

Sticky, golden-yellow sap from
conifer trees can sometimes harden
and crystallize to form a hard organic
gem called amber. According to the
ancient Greeks, this substance
contained trapped sunlight.

Amber is actually a fossil. Like preserved pollen
or a pinecone, it is part of an ancient tree that lived
millions of years ago. Amber forms from hardened
resin that oozes from inside a tree. **Raw amber**
can be found on the sea floor in large, rough-
shaped **amber nodules** and **pebbles**. Water

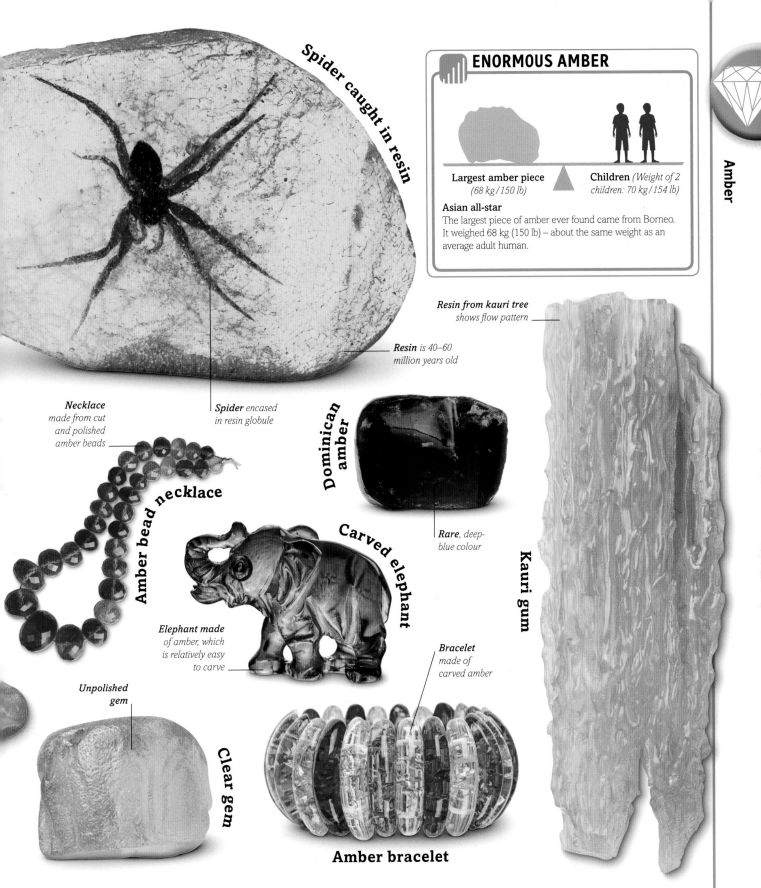

Spider caught in resin

ENORMOUS AMBER

Largest amber piece *(68 kg / 150 lb)*

Children *(Weight of 2 children: 70 kg / 154 lb)*

Asian all-star
The largest piece of amber ever found came from Borneo. It weighed 68 kg (150 lb) – about the same weight as an average adult human.

Resin from kauri tree shows flow pattern

Resin is 40–60 million years old

Necklace made from cut and polished amber beads

Spider encased in resin globule

Amber bead necklace

Dominican amber

Rare, deep-blue colour

Kauri gum

Carved elephant

Elephant made of amber, which is relatively easy to carve

Bracelet made of carved amber

Unpolished gem

Clear gem

Amber bracelet

caught in the resin creates a "**sun-spangled**" effect. Amber may even contain trapped fossils. Most amber comes from Russia and Scandinavia, but there are deposits of amber in Asia, Africa, and the Caribbean. This gem is made into **polished beads** for jewellery or carved into decorative ornaments. Amber mainly comes in warm sunset and honey colours, but it can also be green, red, and even blue-coloured **Dominican amber**. King Frederick I of Prussia liked amber so much he created an **Amber Room** out of it – which was called the "Eighth Wonder of the World".

Opal

Blue opal deposit in cavity in ironstone rock

Round-cut gemstone

Glasslike lustre

Fire opal gem

Fire opal

Boulder opal

Rose opal

Opaque surface

Rough opal

Single opal set in gold

Victorian ring

Uncut, unshaped opal

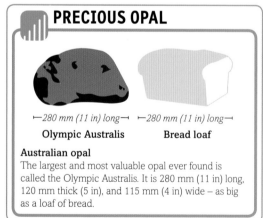

PRECIOUS OPAL

├─ *280 mm (11 in) long* ─┤   ├─ *280 mm (11 in) long* ─┤

Olympic Australis   **Bread loaf**

Australian opal
The largest and most valuable opal ever found is called the Olympic Australis. It is 280 mm (11 in) long, 120 mm thick (5 in), and 115 mm (4 in) wide – as big as a loaf of bread.

Opal is a precious stone made from hardened silica gel. It is a mineraloid and lacks a regular internal crystal structure. Even though it is not a true mineral, its swirling colours and pearly sheen have been prized since ancient times.

Common opal, often called **potch opal**, comes in a variety of colours, including off-whites, dull reds and yellows, and even **rose**. Precious opal is semi-transparent and has a glittering shimmer caused by tiny silica balls that break the light into colours, and make it appear to play over the gem's surface.

Black opal

Play of blue and green in black opal

Rare, dark colour variety

Chocolate opal

Dark, chocolate-brown colour

Roebling opal

The Roebling opal is a **2,585-carat** (517 g / 18.2 oz) gemstone.

Potch opal

Flat, dull surface

Opal pineapple

Crazing cracks reflect light

Square-cut opal

Opal has replaced glauberite crystals

Gilson opal

Artificial opal has the same composition as natural opal

Microscopic cracks, called crazing, also reflect light. The major source for opal today is Ethiopia. Lightning Ridge opal field in New South Wales, Australia, produces the rare **black opal**. **Fire opal** is the the most prized form. **Boulder opal** forms inside rocks, where circulating, mineral-rich fluids deposit silica in cavities and cracks. Precious opal also replaces bone, wood, and other hard parts, to form opalized fossils. The massive **Roebling opal** – an extraordinary specimen found in Nevada, USA – was deposited in a hole where a buried tree rotted away.

Decorative stones

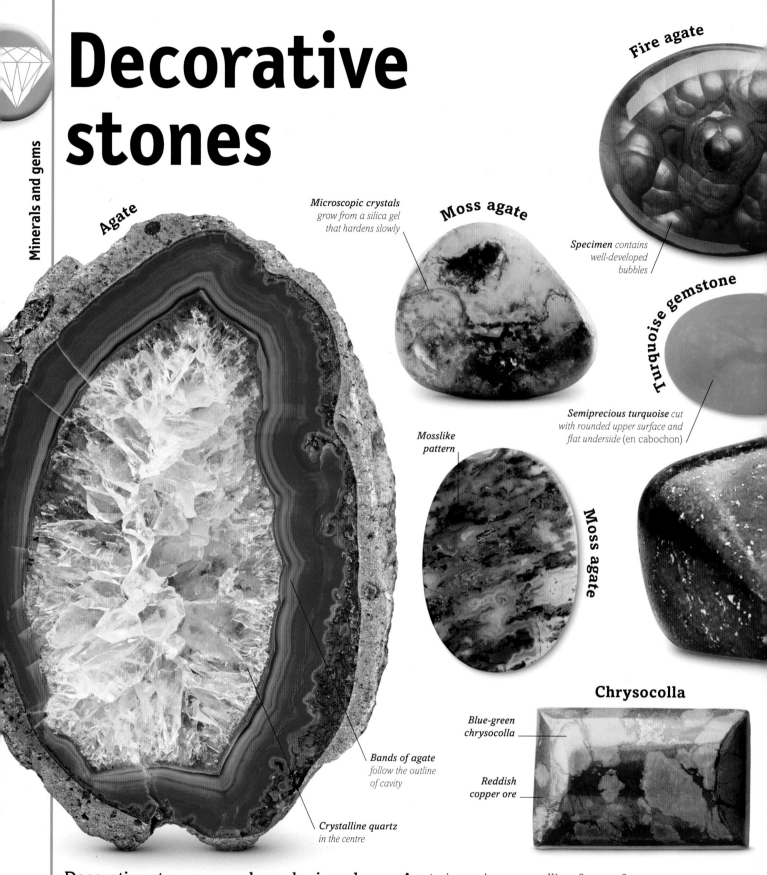

Fire agate

Agate

Moss agate

Microscopic crystals grow from a silica gel that hardens slowly

Specimen contains well-developed bubbles

Turquoise gemstone

Semiprecious turquoise cut with rounded upper surface and flat underside (en cabochon)

Mosslike pattern

Moss agate

Bands of agate follow the outline of cavity

Crystalline quartz in the centre

Chrysocolla

Blue-green chrysocolla

Reddish copper ore

Decorative stones are coloured minerals that look beautiful when polished. Although only a few are rare, they are at times more highly valued than precious metals. Turquoise and lapis lazuli were thought to be sacred by ancient cultures.

Agate is a microcrystalline form of quartz, also known as chalcedony. Agates form when circulating, mineral-rich fluids deposit silica in cavities in the rock. Quartz is deposited around the inside surface and builds up in layers that follow the shape of the cavity. When sliced, it

Azurite heart

Vein of *blue-green malachite* in deep blue azurite crystal

Serpentine

Specimen has a greasy lustre

Dumortierite

Polished surface

Ancient Buddhists thought **lapis lazuli** drove away **evil thoughts**.

Moonstone

Polished pebble

Unakite

Sodalite

White veins of calcite

Green colour comes *from the mineral epidote*

Lapis lazuli

Shimmery iridescent play of colours on surface

Labradorite

Goldlike flecks are actually tiny inclusions of pyrite

Polished sardonyx

Bands of brown-red sard and white chalcedony

gives a banded appearance. Impurities give agate lovely colours, such as **fire agate**, which gets its reddish-brown colour from hematite. Manganese oxides and chlorite make the greenish markings in **moss agate**. **Lapis lazuli** is a precious stone whose main component – the mineral lazurite –

gives it an intense blue colour. Just like **turquoise**, lapis lazuli was highly prized in ancient times. Precious, apple-coloured **serpentine** can be mistaken for jade, but it is much softer. **Moonstone** and **labradorite** are both feldspar gemstones used for jewellery and ornaments.

121

FOSSILS

Fossils

A fossil is a remnant, impression, or trace of an organism that once lived on Earth. Typically, after the organism dies, the soft parts decompose, leaving only the hard parts – the shell, teeth, bone, or wood. Buried in layers of sediment, they gradually turn to stone. The most common fossils found are of plants or animals that once lived in a sea or lake.

Dorsal fin

Priscacara liops fossil

Preserved in ash ❯ This complete *Priscacara liops* skeleton was recovered from the Palaeogene lake bed that covered much of western Wyoming, USA. Fine volcanic ash fell into the lake and smothered the fish, then buried and preserved its skeleton.

Spine

Eye socket

Recent relative ❯ *Priscacara liops* is an extinct species of fish from the middle of the Palaeogene period, 66–23 million years ago (MYA). Similar to a modern-day perch, it was around 15 cm (6 in) in length and had strong, protective spines on its back and tail.

Types of fossils

Preserved soft tissue
• Soft tissue can be preserved in substances such as amber (insect) or ice (woolly mammoth).

From wood to stone
• Water deposits minerals into the pores of a shell or the cells of a piece of wood, fossilizing the remains.

Leaving an impression
• Sediment buries an object, such as a leaf. The leaf decays as the sediment hardens, but leaves its imprint.

Natural cast
• Some organisms, such as shells, can be fossilized in an entirely unaltered state.

Trace fossil
• Some living things leave traces behind them, such as footprints, preserved in rock.

GEOLOGICAL TIME

Earth's geological timescale is divided into divisions called "periods". Multiple periods form a division called an "era".

Pre-Cambrian (4.6 BYA–541 MYA)	EARLY EARTH
Cambrian (541–485 MYA)	PALAEOZOIC ERA
Ordovician (485–444 MYA)	
Silurian (444–419 MYA)	
Devonian (419–359 MYA)	
Carboniferous (359–298 MYA)	
Permian (298–252 MYA)	
Triassic (252–201 MYA)	MESOZOIC ERA
Jurassic (201–145 MYA)	
Cretaceous (145–66 MYA)	
Palaeogene (66–23 MYA)	CENOZOIC ERA
Neogene (23–2.6 MYA)	
Quaternary (2.6 MYA–present)	

Life in the ancient seas

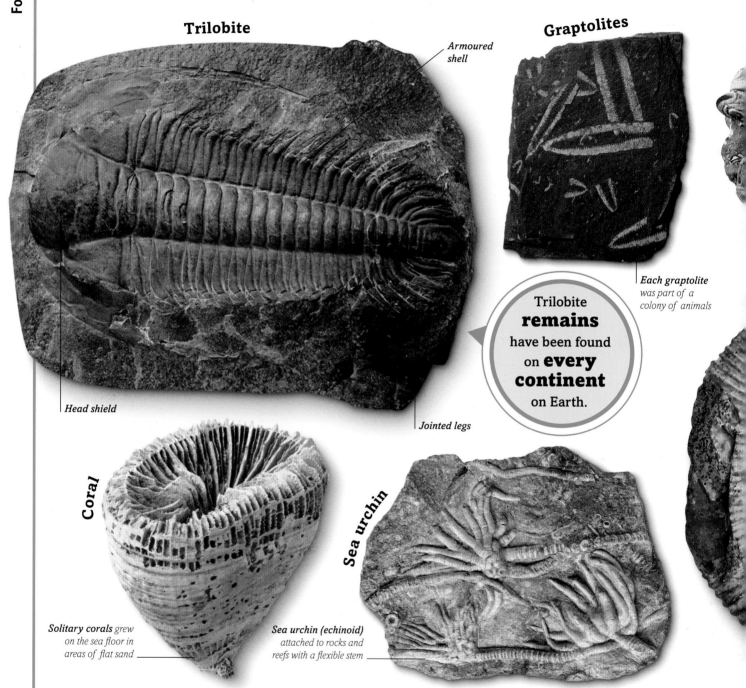

Trilobite

Armoured shell

Graptolites

Each graptolite *was part of a colony of animals*

Trilobite **remains** have been found on **every continent** on Earth.

Head shield

Jointed legs

Coral

Sea urchin

Solitary corals *grew on the sea floor in areas of flat sand*

Sea urchin (echinoid) *attached to rocks and reefs with a flexible stem*

The world's oldest fossils are tiny, floating, bacterialike cells that lived in the oceans about 3.8 billion years ago. Over millions of years, more complex sea creatures gradually evolved. These animals were invertebrates (animals without backbones).

The most common fossils found today are the remains of the animals that lived in the ancient seas that once covered most of Earth. Creatures lurking on the sea bed were the most likely to fossilize because they would become buried in mud before they rotted away. Bacteria, worms,

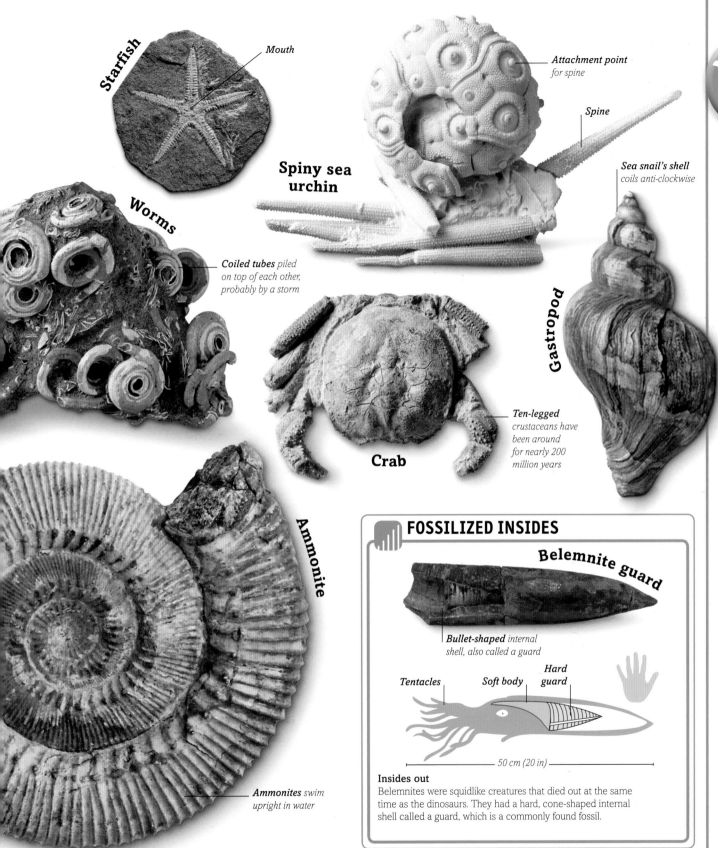

Starfish

Mouth

Spiny sea urchin

Attachment point
for spine

Spine

Sea snail's shell
coils anti-clockwise

Worms

Coiled tubes piled
on top of each other,
probably by a storm

Gastropod

Ten-legged
crustaceans have
been around
for nearly 200
million years

Crab

Ammonite

Ammonites swim
upright in water

FOSSILIZED INSIDES

Belemnite guard

Bullet-shaped internal
shell, also called a guard

Tentacles   Soft body   Hard
                            guard

—— *50 cm (20 in)* ——

Insides out
Belemnites were squidlike creatures that died out at the same
time as the dinosaurs. They had a hard, cone-shaped internal
shell called a guard, which is a commonly found fossil.

jellyfish, and other animals with soft bodies do not
fossilize well. What looks like fossil **worms** are,
in fact, the hard tubes in which the animals lived.
Invertebrates with protective shells and hard inner
parts preserve better, such as the **trilobites** that
lived between 520–250 million years ago, roaming
across the sea bed protected by their outer shell.
Graptolites, like **coral**, were homes for colonies
of small soft-bodied animals. **Crabs, starfish,** and
sea urchins look similar to present-day species
found in rock pools. **Ammonites** are the shells
of ancestors of the octopus and squid.

127

Fossil fish

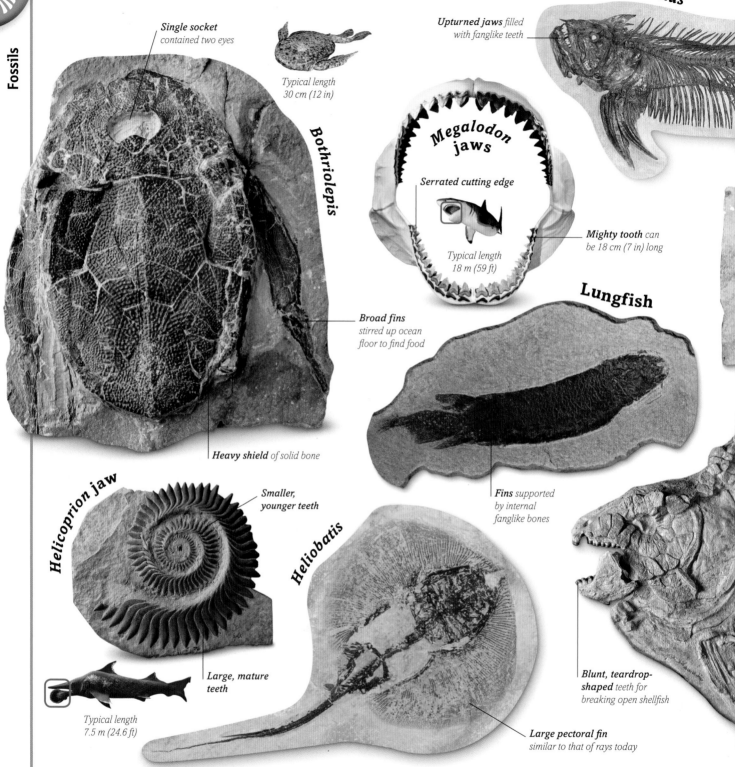

Xiphactinus

Single socket *contained two eyes*

Typical length 30 cm (12 in)

Bothriolepis

Upturned jaws *filled with fanglike teeth*

Megalodon jaws

Serrated cutting edge

Typical length 18 m (59 ft)

Mighty tooth *can be 18 cm (7 in) long*

Broad fins *stirred up ocean floor to find food*

Lungfish

Heavy shield *of solid bone*

Fins *supported by internal fanglike bones*

Helicoprion jaw

Smaller, younger teeth

Heliobatis

Large, mature teeth

Typical length 7.5 m (24.6 ft)

Blunt, teardrop-shaped *teeth for breaking open shellfish*

Large pectoral fin *similar to that of rays today*

The first vertebrates – animals with backbones – were fish. A backbone, or vertebral column, supports a bony skeleton inside the body. Amphibians, reptiles, mammals, and birds are all vertebrates descended from fish.

The first fish were jawless. They sifted through the ooze and soft sediment on the sea floor, sucking up tasty morsels. Fish developed the first bones, cartilage (the tough, flexible tissue in your joints), and enamelled teeth. Early jawed fish, such as **Bothriolepis** had head and fins

128

Deep tail powered fish to a top speed of 60 km/h (37 mph)

Fossil of prey inside stomach

Backbone built of bony vertebrae

Coelacanth

Fossilized coelacanth from 66 million years ago

Mene rhombea

The coelacanth was thought to be **extinct**, but was rediscovered in **1938**.

Long fins helped fish to manoeuvre in water

Thick, diamond-shaped scales

Lepidotes maximus

Seahorse

Curled tail grips onto seaweed

covered in heavy bony armour, to serve as protection from the hungry mouths of predators roving the seas. Instead of bone, the skeletons of sharks and rays are made of cartilage. The sharklike **Helicoprion** had 180 teeth set in a strange spiral, like a circular saw. Rays such as **Heliobatis** date from around 56 million years ago and are nearly flat. Their whiplike tail had up to three wickedly barbed spikes loaded with poison. But perhaps scariest of all was **Megalodon**, at 18 m (59 ft) long, the largest shark that has ever lived.

Plant fossils

Cooksonia

Slender stalk branches only once

Capsule containing spores

Lichen

Fossil made up of layers between 1 and 2 mm (0.03–0.07 in) thick

Oil-producing bodies stop liverworts drying out in the Sun

Liverwort

Lepidodendron

Bark has a scalelike surface

Archaeopteris

Treelike form, with trunk and branches

Fernlike leaves

Trigonocarpus

Fossilized seed

A living fossil, **ginkgo** has remained unchanged for **270** million years.

Ginkgo

Fan-shaped leaves

The evolution of the first land plants was a major event in Earth's history. It cleared the way for the development of animal life on land, and was the starting point for the wide variety of plants we see today.

All plants convert sunlight into sugar (a process called photosynthesis) and use this energy to build their bodies. The earliest plants to learn this trick were algae (microscopic plankton and seaweed) living in the oceans. Hardy **liverworts** and **lichens** first appeared on land around 450 million years

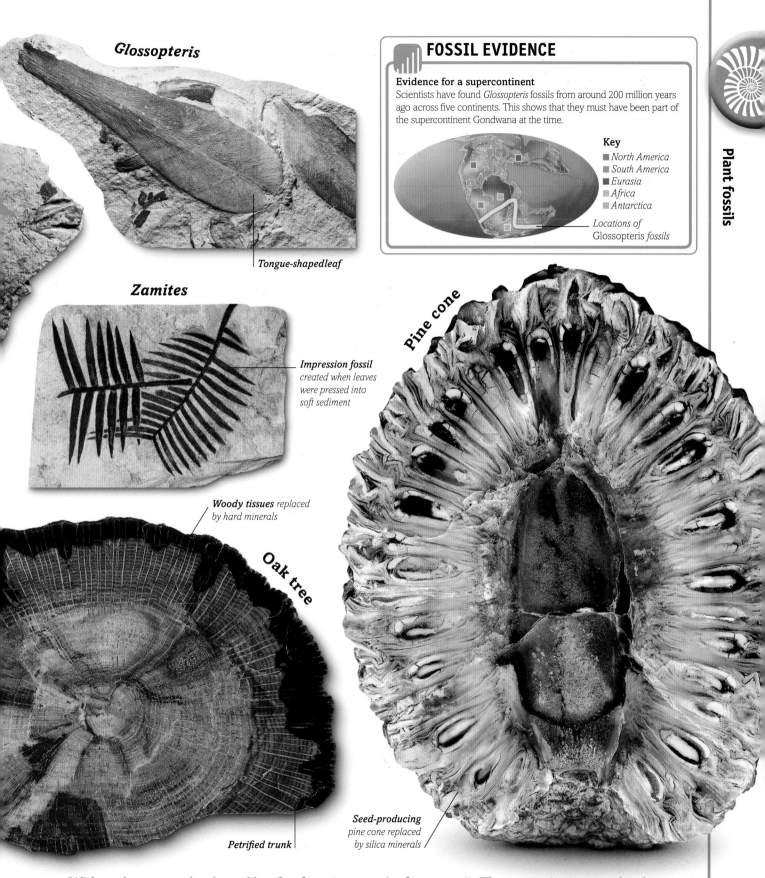

Glossopteris

Tongue-shapedleaf

Zamites

Impression fossil
*created when leaves
were pressed into
soft sediment*

Pine cone

Woody tissues *replaced
by hard minerals*

Oak tree

Petrified trunk

Seed-producing
*pine cone replaced
by silica minerals*

ago. With no leaves, early plants like **Cooksonia** transported fluids around their bodies using internal tubes. Clusters of light-sensitive cells developed into leaves around 360 million years ago. Prehistoric swamps were full of mosslike plants, such as **Lepidodendron**, and tree ferns like **Archaeopteris**. They grew into trees, thanks to woody tissues that supported their weight, and spread by producing spores. Palmlike cycads, such as **Zamites**, developed the first seeds, which were able to survive drought. Flowering plants, such as the **oak**, evolved around 130 million years ago.

131

TREES OF STONE
The light of the morning Sun catches on loglike pieces of solid rock lying on the ground as though they were trunks sawn for firewood. These are the petrified remains of a prehistoric forest in Arizona's Painted Desert, USA. Petrification is a process by which organic material turns to stone over time. Minerals, which replaced the trees' organic matter and turned it into stone, glow in warm red and brown colours.

About 225 million years ago, the southern state of Arizona in the USA stood on the southwestern edge of a supercontinent called Pangaea. Situated near to the equator, its humid climate bred a huge variety of ferns, cycads, ginkgoes, and tall conifer trees. Streams flowing from the mountains across the plains passed through these large forests, depositing silt and burying fallen trees and vegetation. Every so often, volcanoes would deposit ash over the region. Groundwater dissolved silica from the ash and washed through the buried trunks as it trickled through the wet sediment. Slowly, quartz crystals grew inside the trees, replacing the organic structures of the wood, until it became totally petrified.

The first land animals

Eusthenopteron foordi

Ichthyostega limb

Like all tetrapods, this amphibian ancestor has a one-two-many pattern of bones in its limbs (one in the upper arm, two in the forearm, and many in the hand)

Typical length
3.3 m (10.8 ft)

Eryops

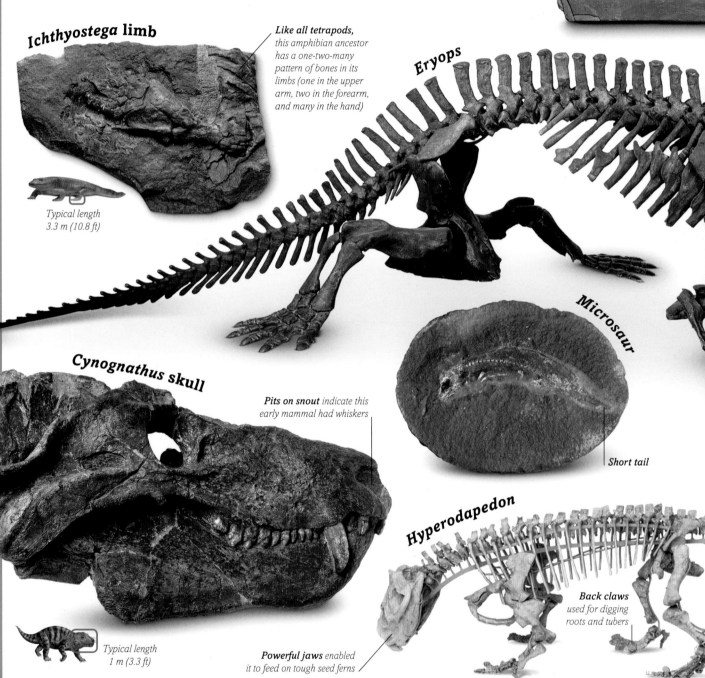

Cynognathus skull

Pits on snout indicate this early mammal had whiskers

Microsaur

Short tail

Hyperodapedon

Back claws used for digging roots and tubers

Typical length
1 m (3.3 ft)

Powerful jaws enabled it to feed on tough seed ferns

About 395 million years ago, tetrapods (animals with four limbs) evolved from fish. These would be the first vertebrates to move from water to land. The study of fossils has helped scientists to understand how animals adapted to live in this new environment.

To survive on land, animals need lungs for breathing air and limbs for walking. This means a skeleton to support their body weight and limbs strong enough to move around. About 385 million years ago, lobe-finned "fish with legs", such as *Eusthenopteron*, had evolved many of these

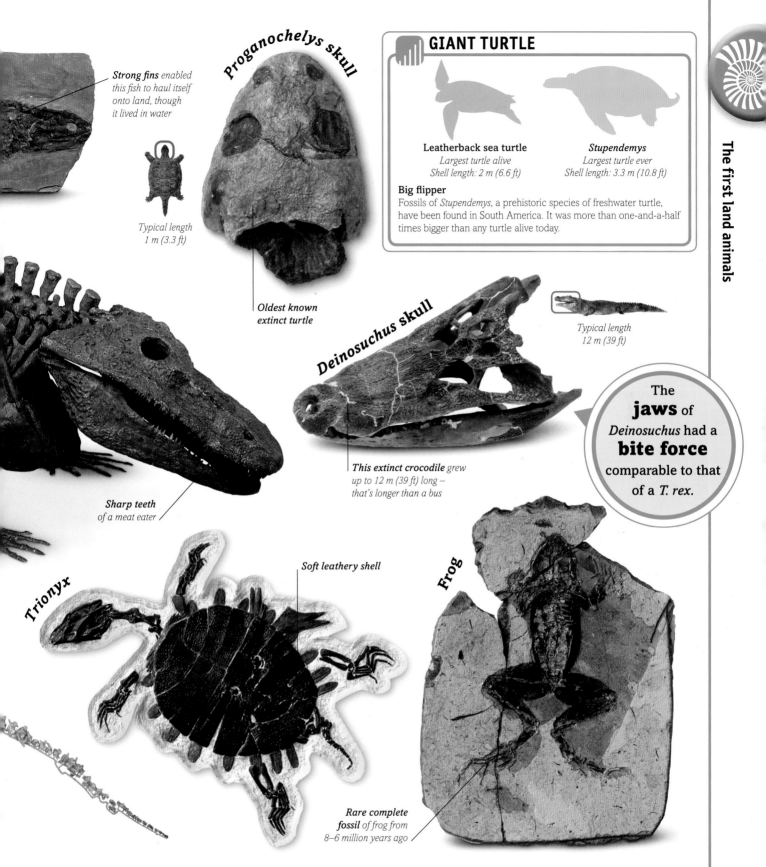

Strong fins enabled this fish to haul itself onto land, though it lived in water

Proganochelys skull

Typical length 1 m (3.3 ft)

Oldest known extinct turtle

GIANT TURTLE

Leatherback sea turtle
*Largest turtle alive
Shell length: 2 m (6.6 ft)*

Stupendemys
*Largest turtle ever
Shell length: 3.3 m (10.8 ft)*

Big flipper
Fossils of *Stupendemys*, a prehistoric species of freshwater turtle, have been found in South America. It was more than one-and-a-half times bigger than any turtle alive today.

Deinosuchus skull

Typical length 12 m (39 ft)

This extinct crocodile grew up to 12 m (39 ft) long — that's longer than a bus

Sharp teeth *of a meat eater*

The **jaws** of *Deinosuchus* had a **bite force** comparable to that of a *T. rex*.

Trionyx

Soft leathery shell

Frog

Rare complete fossil of frog from 8–6 million years ago

features. Halfway between a fish and an amphibian, four-legged **Ichthyostega** was capable of short spells above water, but lived a mostly aquatic life in shallow swamps. **Microsaur** was an early amphibian, with small legs that enabled it to live on land. **Eryops** was happy on dry land, but relied on water for laying and hatching its eggs. Modern amphibians, such as **frogs**, still live semiaquatic lifestyles. Early tetrapods like these evolved to become the ancestors of dinosaurs (**Hyperodapedon**), crocodiles (**Deinosuchus**), and even mammals (**Cynognathus**).

135

Marine reptiles

Long, narrow snout

Pointed head on a long neck

Long jaws suggest this reptile hunted fish

Askeptosaurus

Keichousaurus

Hunting in deep waters required the **biggest eyes** ever seen in vertebrates.

Webbed feet useful for life in the water

Ring of bones around eye socket

Ichthyosaur

Large tail powers streamlined body

The shallow seas of the Jurassic period were full of terrifying monsters. Giant reptiles stalked the waters hunting fish, chasing shellfish, and eating each other. Preserved in fine-grained marine muds, they make beautiful fossils.

Ocean lizards, such as **Askeptosaurus**, were some of the first reptiles to take to the oceans in the Triassic period. Growing up to 2 m (6.6 ft) long and with a strong paddlelike tail, they were swift predators. The nothosaurs were another group of marine reptiles. They included the

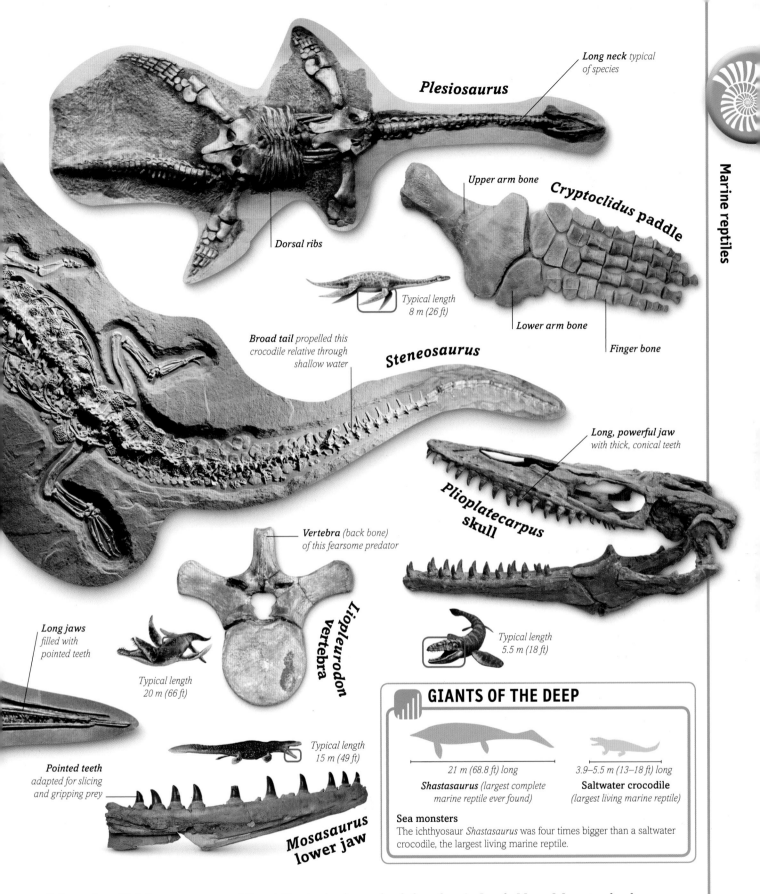

Plesiosaurus

Long neck typical of species

Dorsal ribs

Cryptoclidus paddle

Upper arm bone

Lower arm bone

Finger bone

Typical length
8 m (26 ft)

Broad tail propelled this crocodile relative through shallow water

Steneosaurus

Long, powerful jaw with thick, conical teeth

Plioplatecarpus skull

Vertebra (back bone) of this fearsome predator

Liopleurodon vertebra

Long jaws filled with pointed teeth

Typical length
20 m (66 ft)

Typical length
5.5 m (18 ft)

Pointed teeth adapted for slicing and gripping prey

Typical length
15 m (49 ft)

Mosasaurus lower jaw

GIANTS OF THE DEEP

21 m (68.8 ft) long
Shastasaurus (largest complete marine reptile ever found)

3.9–5.5 m (13–18 ft) long
Saltwater crocodile (largest living marine reptile)

Sea monsters
The ichthyosaur *Shastasaurus* was four times bigger than a saltwater crocodile, the largest living marine reptile.

fish-eating **Keichousaurus** and lived like today's seals, hunting in the water, but coming out to bask in the sunshine on rocks. Meanwhile, "fish-lizard" **ichthyosaur**, shaped like modern sharks and dolphins, torpedoed through the water. Long-necked plesiosaurs, such as **Cryptoclidus**, had the classic Loch Ness Monster look. There were also short-necked ones, such as **Liopleurodon**, which was bigger than a sperm whale. These amazing animals went extinct at the same time as the dinosaurs, 66 million years ago.

Flying reptiles

Toothless beak

Teeth with three cusps helped to slice up prey

Eudimorphodon

Sharp claws helped to grasp

Long wings meant Rhamphorhynchus could ride the wind like an albatross

Rhamphorhynchus

Dimorphodon

Dimorphodon's body length was almost three times the size of its head

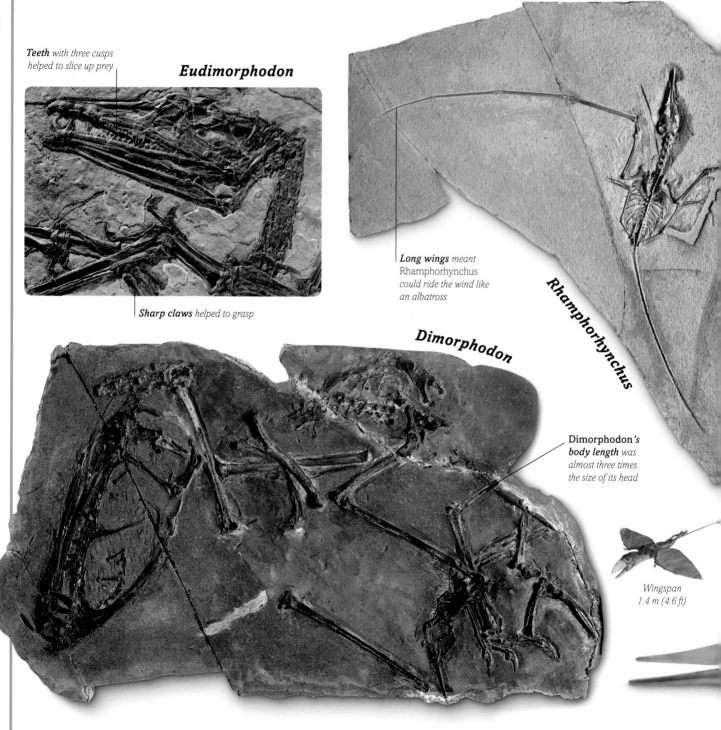

Wingspan 1.4 m (4.6 ft)

Swooping and soaring on leathery skin, pterosaurs, or winged lizards, ruled the Jurassic skies. Before birds evolved, they were the only flying vertebrates. They were related to the dinosaurs and lived between 225 and 66 million years ago.

One of the oldest known flying reptiles is *Eudimorphodon* from 210 million years ago. This small pterosaur had a wingspan of 1 m (3.3 ft). An agile flier, it may have hunted insects on the wing. *Rhamphorhynchus* had a long tail and wings but a short head.

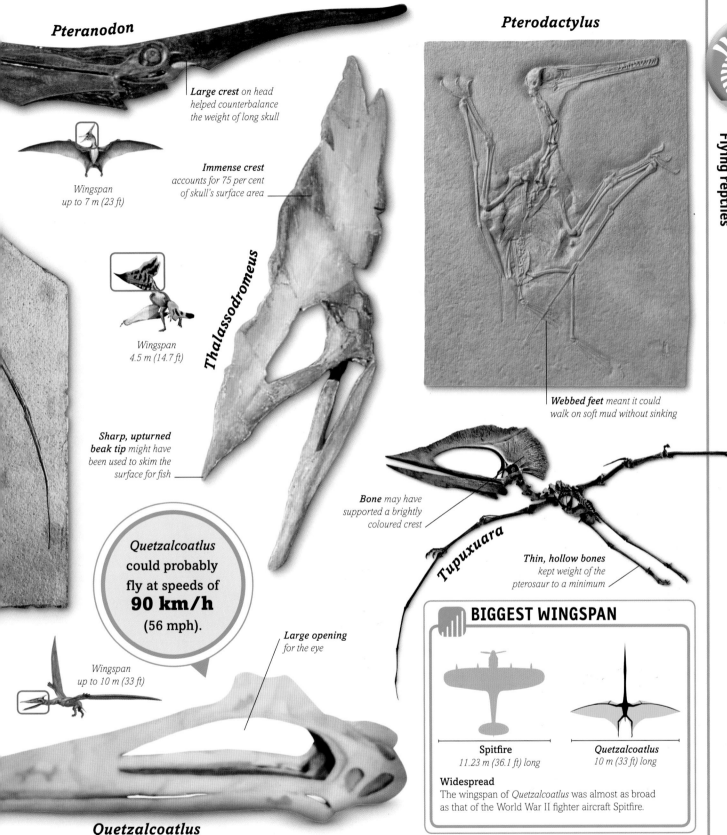

Pteranodon

Large crest on head helped counterbalance the weight of long skull

Wingspan up to 7 m (23 ft)

Pterodactylus

Webbed feet meant it could walk on soft mud without sinking

Immense crest accounts for 75 per cent of skull's surface area

Thalassodromeus

Wingspan 4.5 m (14.7 ft)

Sharp, upturned beak tip might have been used to skim the surface for fish

Tupuxuara

Bone may have supported a brightly coloured crest

Thin, hollow bones kept weight of the pterosaur to a minimum

Quetzalcoatlus could probably fly at speeds of **90 km/h** (56 mph).

Wingspan up to 10 m (33 ft)

Large opening for the eye

Quetzalcoatlus

BIGGEST WINGSPAN

Spitfire
11.23 m (36.1 ft) long

Quetzalcoatlus
10 m (33 ft) long

Widespread
The wingspan of *Quetzalcoatlus* was almost as broad as that of the World War II fighter aircraft Spitfire.

Pteranodon was huge, with wings that stretched 7 m (23 ft). Pterosaurs such as **Thalassodromeus** and **Pterodactylus** had short tails, long limbs, large heads and necks, and were masters of flight. Their wings were a flap of skin stretched between a very long fourth finger and rear limbs. On these leathery wings, they wheeled out over the ocean, diving and snapping fish out of the water. The biggest pterosaur was **Quetzalcoatlus**, with a wingspan around 10 m (33 ft) in length.

Meat-eating monsters

Fossilized nest *of Oviraptor eggs*

Coprolites

Undigested scraps of bones *in this dropping (coprolite) show what the dinosaur ate*

Megalosaurus footprint

Dinosaur footprints *in the rocks help us understand how they moved*

Typical length 9 m (29.5 ft)

Long tail *was supported by strong muscles*

Deinonychus skull

Curved and serrated teeth *helped to slice prey's flesh*

Typical length 3 m (9.8 ft)

T. rex could swallow about **230 kg** (500 lb) of flesh in **one bite**.

When people first discovered dinosaur fossils they thought they must be the bones of living animals. But as they studied the jigsaw of bones, they began to realize that fossils were the remains of animals that had long been extinct.

The first fossil hunters named these animals dinosaurs, which means "terrible lizard". *Megalosaurus* was the first to be identified, and had the long, curved teeth of a meat-eater. One of the most powerful land predators that has ever lived was *Tyrannosaurus*. Agile and

Baryonyx skull

Remains of dinosaurs found in *Baryonyx*'s **stomach** show it ate land animals as well.

Typical length 2 m (6.6 ft)

Baryonyx teeth are similar to those of the fish-eating crocodile

Velociraptor claw

Long, sharp claw

Typical length 9.5 m (31 ft)

Tyrannosaurus rex

Jaws designed to crush bone

Allosaurus

Forward-pointing eyes *gave this hunter excellent vision*

Slender neck

Sharp, serrated teeth

Two-fingered forearm *gripped prey, but was too short to reach the mouth*

Coelophysis

Short, fourth toe *on the inner side of each foot*

Hollow limb bones, *like those of birds*

able to run fast on two legs, it is *Tyrannosaurus*'s bone-crushing teeth that made it such a fearsome hunter. The teeth of **Allosaurus** were more like knife blades, while those of **Baryonyx** were pointed for piercing the slippery skin of fish. Not all the most vicious meat-eaters were big.

Coelophysis was a lean, lightweight hunter about 3 m (9.8 ft) long. **Velociraptor** was even smaller, but had killer claws for attacking prey such as small dinosaurs, mammals, and lizards. *Velociraptor* was covered in feathers but could not fly, and is an ancient relative of birds.

Plant-eaters

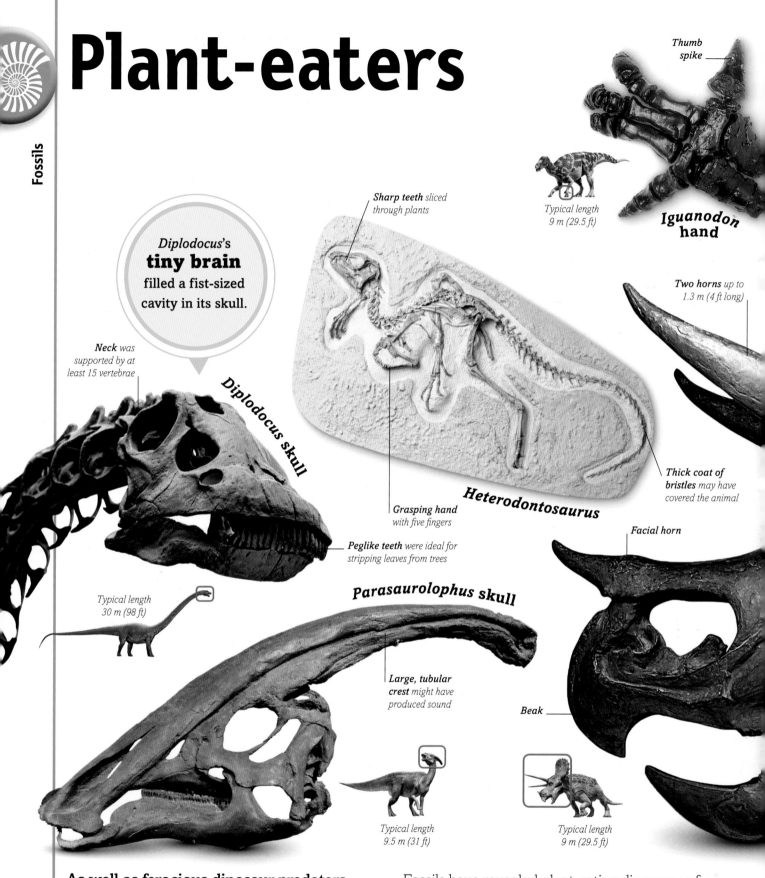

Thumb spike

Iguanodon hand

Typical length
9 m (29.5 ft)

Sharp teeth sliced through plants

Diplodocus's **tiny brain** filled a fist-sized cavity in its skull.

Neck was supported by at least 15 vertebrae

Diplodocus skull

Heterodontosaurus

Grasping hand with five fingers

Peglike teeth were ideal for stripping leaves from trees

Typical length
30 m (98 ft)

Two horns up to
1.3 m (4 ft long)

Thick coat of bristles may have covered the animal

Facial horn

Parasaurolophus skull

Large, tubular crest might have produced sound

Beak

Typical length
9.5 m (31 ft)

Typical length
9 m (29.5 ft)

As well as ferocious dinosaur predators, much gentler giants also once roamed Earth. The largest and longest dinosaurs were plant-eaters. These beasts would have had to graze almost constantly to consume enough energy to keep their bodies working.

Fossils have revealed plant-eating dinosaurs of all shapes and sizes, and with curious features and habits. Many, including **Triceratops**, had a beak to tear at leaves and stems. **Euoplocephalus** was a solitary animal with thick armour and a mighty tail club to swing at attackers, while

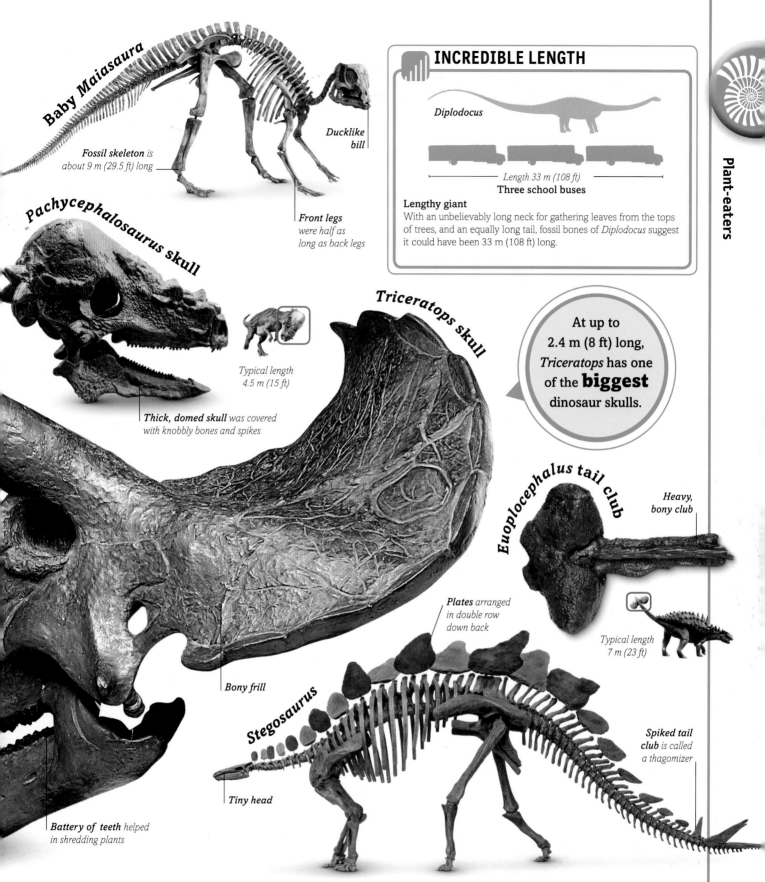

Baby Maiasaura

Fossil skeleton is about 9 m (29.5 ft) long

Ducklike bill

Front legs were half as long as back legs

Pachycephalosaurus skull

Typical length 4.5 m (15 ft)

Thick, domed skull *was covered with knobbly bones and spikes*

INCREDIBLE LENGTH

Diplodocus

Length 33 m (108 ft)
Three school buses

Lengthy giant
With an unbelievably long neck for gathering leaves from the tops of trees, and an equally long tail, fossil bones of *Diplodocus* suggest it could have been 33 m (108 ft) long.

At up to 2.4 m (8 ft) long, *Triceratops* has one of the **biggest** dinosaur skulls.

Triceratops skull

Bony frill

Battery of teeth *helped in shredding plants*

Euoplocephalus tail club

Heavy, bony club

Typical length 7 m (23 ft)

Plates *arranged in double row down back*

Stegosaurus

Tiny head

Spiked tail club is called a thagomizer

Maiasaura and *Iguanodon* sought safety in numbers and grazed in herds. Sometimes scientists can only guess how dinosaurs behaved. Were the enormous plates along the back of *Stegosaurus* for show, or to make it look bigger? *Pachycephalosaurus* had a domed skull at least 20 cm (8 in) thick. Some think this may be because rival males had head-butting competitions to decide which one was dominant. And perhaps *Parasaurolophus* was able to communicate using its tubular crest to produce a trumpeting sound, like an elephant?

Dino birds

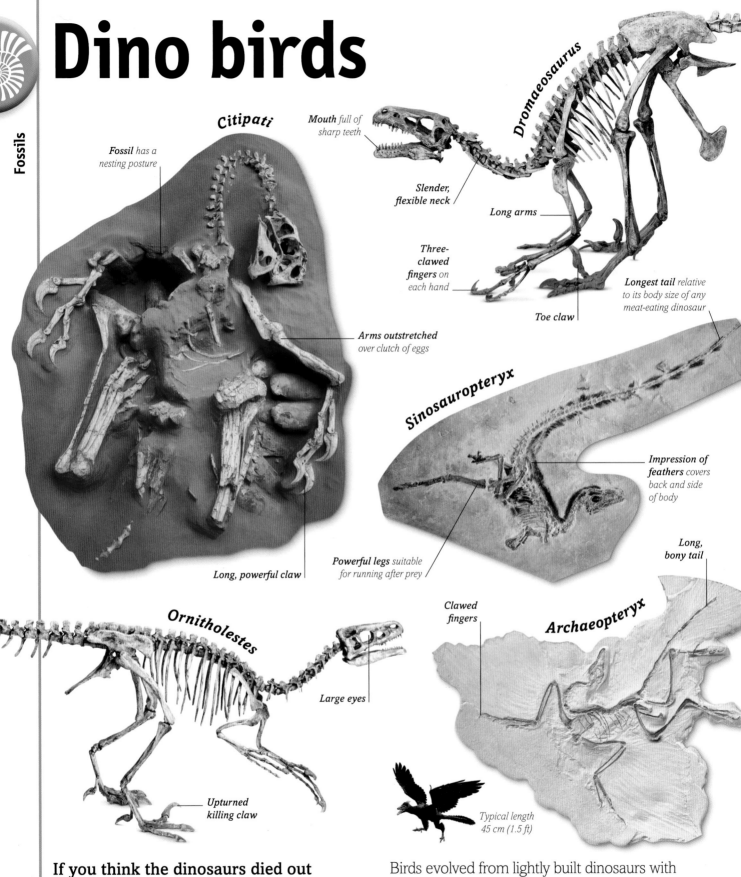

Citipati

Fossil has a nesting posture

Mouth full of sharp teeth

Dromaeosaurus

Slender, flexible neck

Long arms

Three-clawed fingers on each hand

Arms outstretched over clutch of eggs

Toe claw

Longest tail relative to its body size of any meat-eating dinosaur

Sinosauropteryx

Impression of feathers covers back and side of body

Long, powerful claw

Powerful legs suitable for running after prey

Ornitholestes

Large eyes

Clawed fingers

Long, bony tail

Archaeopteryx

Upturned killing claw

Typical length 45 cm (1.5 ft)

If you think the dinosaurs died out 66 million years ago, you had better think again. There are so many similarities between theropod dinosaurs and birds that scientists think theropods were the ancestors of birds.

Birds evolved from lightly built dinosaurs with raptorlike claws, such as **Dromaeosaurus**. Emu-sized **Citipati** fossils are often found sitting on eggs. Like in birds, this brooding behaviour used the warmth of the body to hatch the eggs. Turkey-sized **Sinosauropteryx** was the first

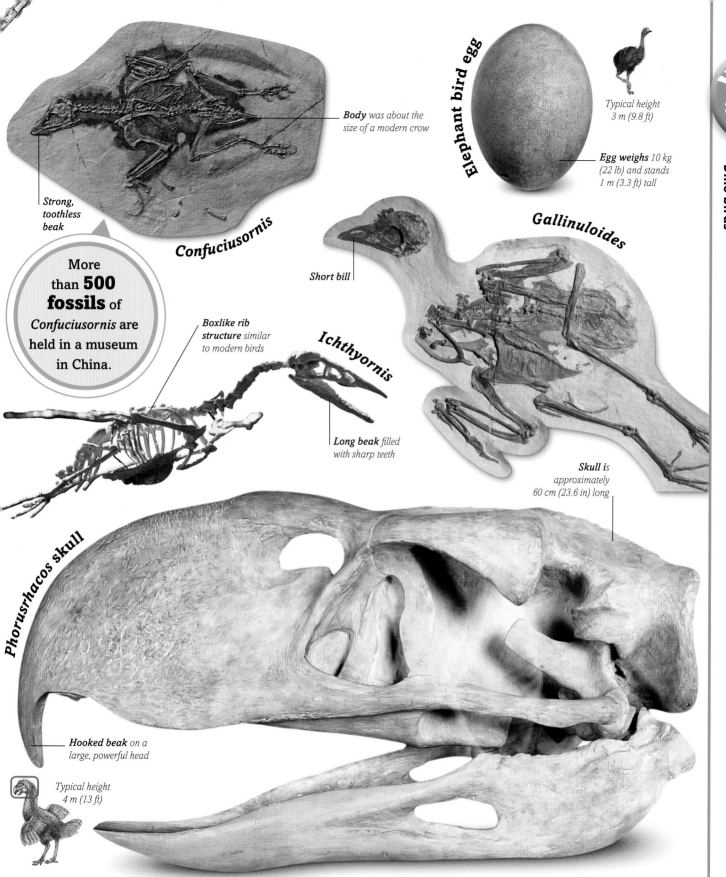

Body was about the size of a modern crow

Strong, toothless beak

Confuciusornis

More than **500 fossils** of *Confuciusornis* are held in a museum in China.

Elephant bird egg

Typical height 3 m (9.8 ft)

Egg weighs 10 kg (22 lb) and stands 1 m (3.3 ft) tall

Short bill

Gallinuloides

Boxlike rib structure similar to modern birds

Ichthyornis

Long beak filled with sharp teeth

Skull is approximately 60 cm (23.6 in) long

Phorusrhacos skull

Hooked beak on a large, powerful head

Typical height 4 m (13 ft)

dinosaur to be found with feathers. Colour pigments trapped in the feathers even show that it had dark reddish and light stripes along its tail. *Archaeopteryx*, from 150 million years ago, has a mix of both reptilian and birdlike features. It had flight-ready, feathered wings like birds, but a toothy beak, clawed fingers on the wing, and a long, bony tail, like dinosaurs. A later bird, *Ichthyornis*, was the Cretaceous equivalent of a seagull, and would fly over the water looking for fish. Most modern birds are small "songbirds", a long way from flightless giants, such as *Phorusrhacos*.

MICRORAPTOR
This beautifully preserved fossil *Microraptor* from Liaoning Province, China, shows off the remains of its thick plumage of feathers. There was something special about these feathers, however. Unlike the body coverings of other feathered dinosaurs, these feathers were not for warmth. They were long, slender, aerodynamic, and built for one purpose – gliding.

This tiny raptor dinosaur lived 130 million years ago in a dense forest. *Microraptor* went one better than modern birds – with feathered front and back legs, it had no less than four wings! It was a glider, lacking the muscles for powered flight. The slim, off-centred feathers had microscopic hooks called barbules linking each to the next to form a smooth flight surface.

Beyond these flight feathers, *Microraptor* had a thick covering of feathers all over its body and running down its tail. A diamond-shaped fan at the end of the tail provided extra stability during flights. In 2012, scientists found pigments at the base of the feathers that showed that, in life, *Microraptor* was dark, with iridescent black feathers like a starling or a jackdaw.

Early mammals

Edges of molars fit together, allowing for efficient chewing

Morganucodon jaw

Typical length
9 cm (3.5 in)

Thylacoleo skull

Typical length
1.5 m (4.9 ft)

Tall vertebrae
(back bones)
allowed for powerful
neck muscles

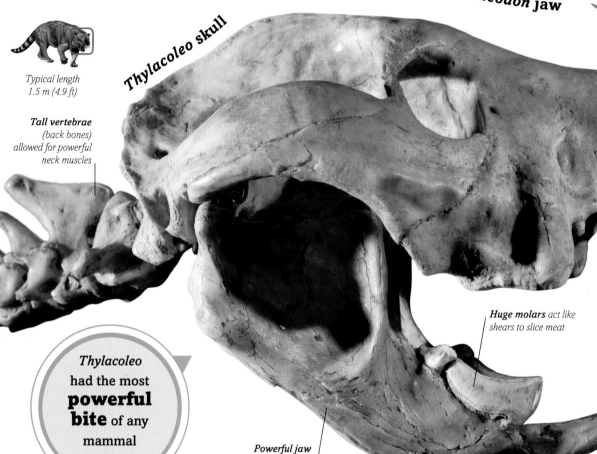

> *Thylacoleo*
> had the most
> **powerful
> bite** of any
> mammal
> ever.

Huge molars act like shears to slice meat

Front incisors
serrated like
a kitchen knife

**Powerful jaw
muscles** attached to
these bone arches

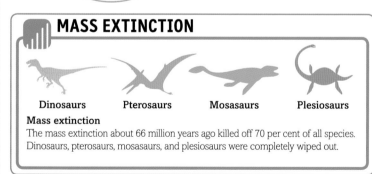

MASS EXTINCTION

Dinosaurs   Pterosaurs   Mosasaurs   Plesiosaurs

Mass extinction
The mass extinction about 66 million years ago killed off 70 per cent of all species. Dinosaurs, pterosaurs, mosasaurs, and plesiosaurs were completely wiped out.

Teeth have many ridges and cusps

Typical length
20 cm (8 in)   *Desmana* jaw

The first mammals – warm-blooded, hairy animals that feed their babies with milk – did not evolve until around 245 million years ago. They only became successful as a group after the dinosaurs went extinct 66 million years ago.

Most mammals give birth to live young, but not all of them do. *Morganucodon*, a mammal ancestor from 200 million years ago, may have produced small, leathery eggs. Some mammals – the platypus, for example – still do. Marsupial mammals, which live in Australasia and the

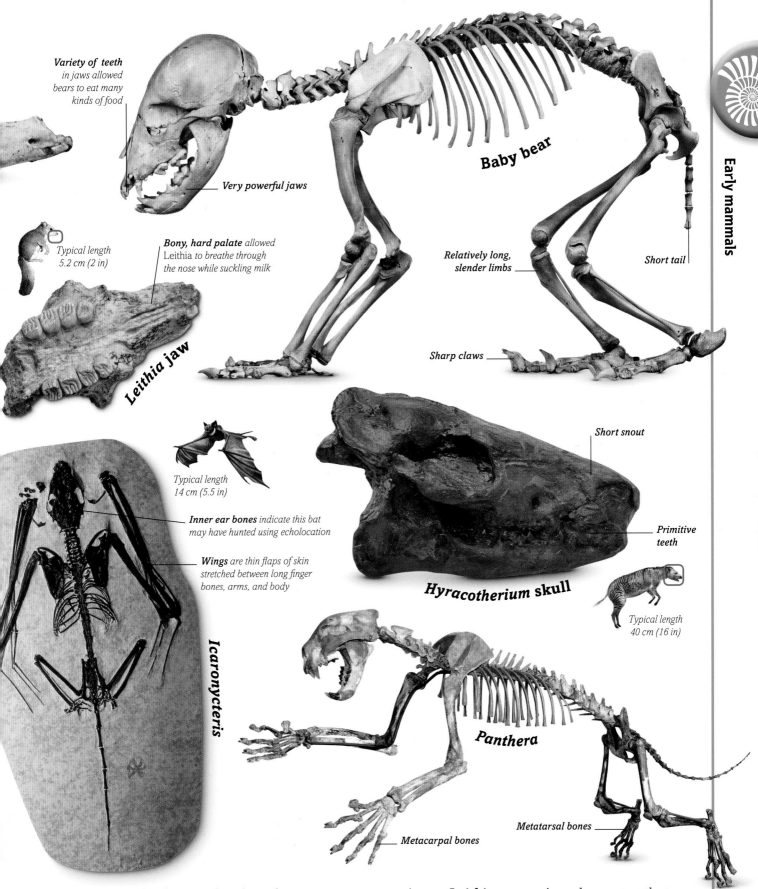

Variety of teeth in jaws allowed bears to eat many kinds of food

Very powerful jaws

Typical length 5.2 cm (2 in)

Bony, hard palate allowed Leithia to breathe through the nose while suckling milk

Leithia jaw

Baby bear

Relatively long, slender limbs

Short tail

Sharp claws

Typical length 14 cm (5.5 in)

Inner ear bones indicate this bat may have hunted using echolocation

Wings are thin flaps of skin stretched between long finger bones, arms, and body

Icaronycteris

Short snout

Primitive teeth

Hyracotherium skull

Typical length 40 cm (16 in)

Panthera

Metacarpal bones

Metatarsal bones

Americas, give birth to undeveloped young, which then develop in the mother's pouch. **Thylacoleo** was a marsupial lion that lived in Australia from 2 million to about 40,000 years ago. Thanks to specialized teeth, it could tear through even the toughest prey in less than a minute. **Leithia** was a giant dormouse that grew as big as a rat. Bats, such as **Icaronycteris**, rose to prominence around 50 million years ago. Carnivores, which include lions and tigers (**Panthera**), dogs, hyenas, **bears**, and marine seals, were another important group.

Mega animals and humans

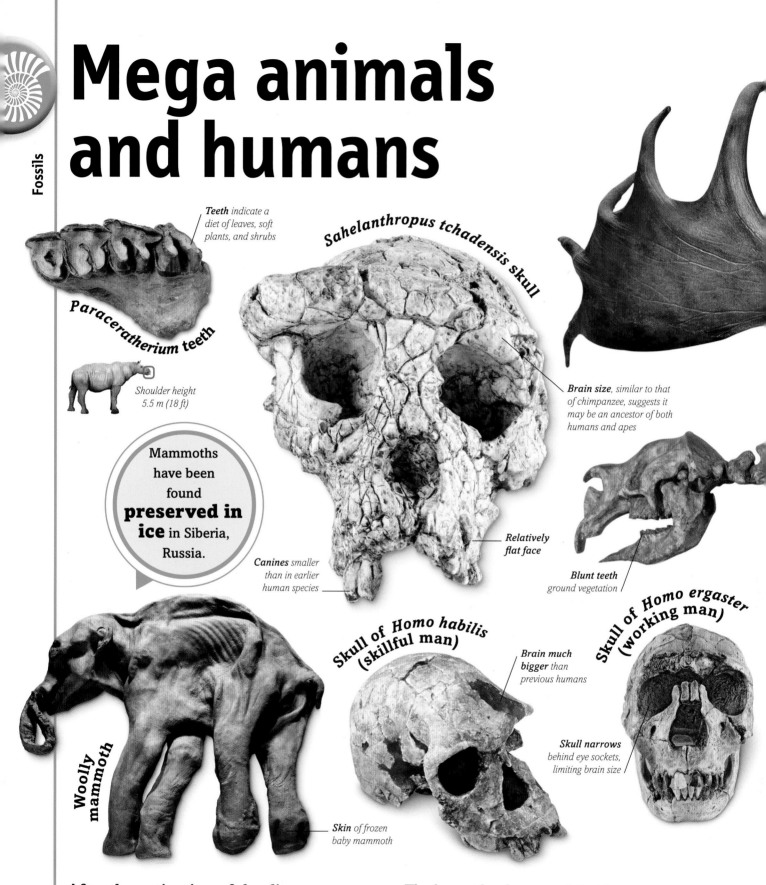

Teeth indicate a diet of leaves, soft plants, and shrubs

Paraceratherium teeth

Sahelanthropus tchadensis skull

Shoulder height 5.5 m (18 ft)

Mammoths have been found **preserved in ice** in Siberia, Russia.

Brain size, similar to that of chimpanzee, suggests it may be an ancestor of both humans and apes

Relatively flat face

Canines smaller than in earlier human species

Blunt teeth ground vegetation

Skull of *Homo ergaster* (working man)

Skull of *Homo habilis* (skillful man)

Brain much bigger than previous humans

Skull narrows behind eye sockets, limiting brain size

Woolly mammoth

Skin of frozen baby mammoth

After the extinction of the dinosaurs, mammals began to dominate life on Earth. As the climate began to cool, modern types of mammal and bird appeared, and the first human ancestors evolved in Africa.

The largest land mammal that has ever existed was *Paraceratherium* – a 20-tonne, giant, hornless rhinoceros that lived more than 30 million years ago. During the last ice age, which lasted from 110,000 to 12,000 years ago, some of the most famous prehistoric animals

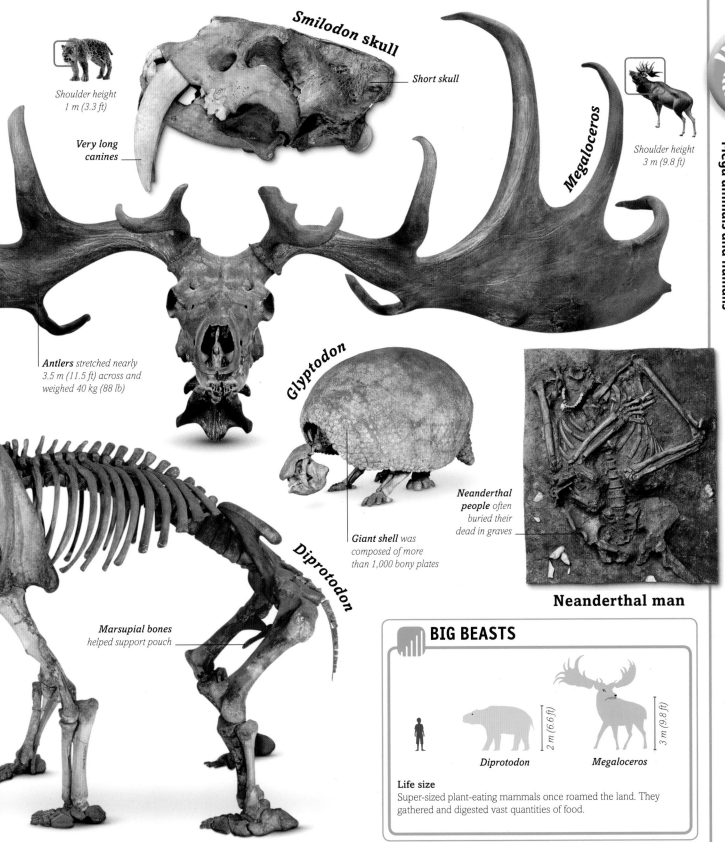

Smilodon skull

Short skull

Very long canines

Shoulder height 1 m (3.3 ft)

Megaloceros

Shoulder height 3 m (9.8 ft)

Antlers *stretched nearly 3.5 m (11.5 ft) across and weighed 40 kg (88 lb)*

Glyptodon

Giant shell *was composed of more than 1,000 bony plates*

Neanderthal people *often buried their dead in graves*

Diprotodon

Marsupial bones *helped support pouch*

Neanderthal man

BIG BEASTS

Diprotodon — 2 m (6.6 ft)

Megaloceros — 3 m (9.8 ft)

Life size
Super-sized plant-eating mammals once roamed the land. They gathered and digested vast quantities of food.

---

appeared. The shaggy-haired **woolly mammoth** roamed the frozen tundra. Many human ancestors and other humanoids, such as *Homo habilis*, *Homo ergaster*, and **Neanderthal man** lived during the same period. Mammoths were often hunted by the sabre-tooth cat, *Smilodon*, with its curved dagger teeth. The fancy antlers of the male Irish elk, *Megaloceros*, designed to impress females of its species, would have made walking in the woods tricky. Australia also had mega animals. *Diprotodon* was an Australian wombat as big as a hippopotamus.

ICE AGE HERDS

On 12 September 1940, four friends were exploring the Lascaux caves in southwestern France when they discovered a new entrance. What they found inside was breathtaking. Nearly 2,000 painted animals were galloping, charging, and running riot over the walls of the caves. This incredible prehistoric art was the work of the early people who lived there nearly 17,300 years ago.

Some 900 animals are recognizable on the walls of the caves at Lascaux, including giant stags, horses, wild bulls, and bison. Some of the paintings are huge. One part of the cave, called the Hall of the Bulls, features a giant bull more than 5 m (16.5 ft) long. The pictures were created using coloured minerals that were crushed to a powder and mixed with animal fat to make natural paints. We can only guess what these haunting images meant to early people. Perhaps they painted them to give thanks for successful hunting? Or perhaps they believed the beasts had magical powers which would bring them luck in future hunts? We will never know.

SHELLS

Shells

A shell is a hard, protective outer layer that has evolved in a wide variety of invertebrates – animals without backbones. Seashells are the most common examples – and most belong to molluscs, such as bivalves and gastropods. The shells of these animals are made from tough protein (called conchiolin) that is hardened by crystals of calcium carbonate, extracted from the sea.

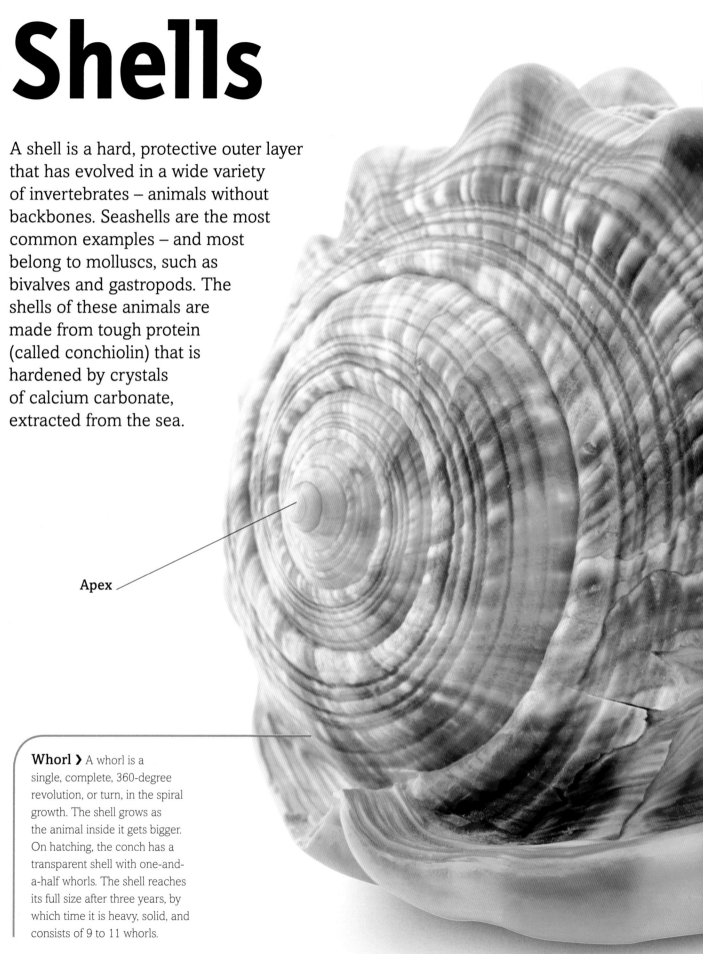

Apex

Whorl › A whorl is a single, complete, 360-degree revolution, or turn, in the spiral growth. The shell grows as the animal inside it gets bigger. On hatching, the conch has a transparent shell with one-and-a-half whorls. The shell reaches its full size after three years, by which time it is heavy, solid, and consists of 9 to 11 whorls.

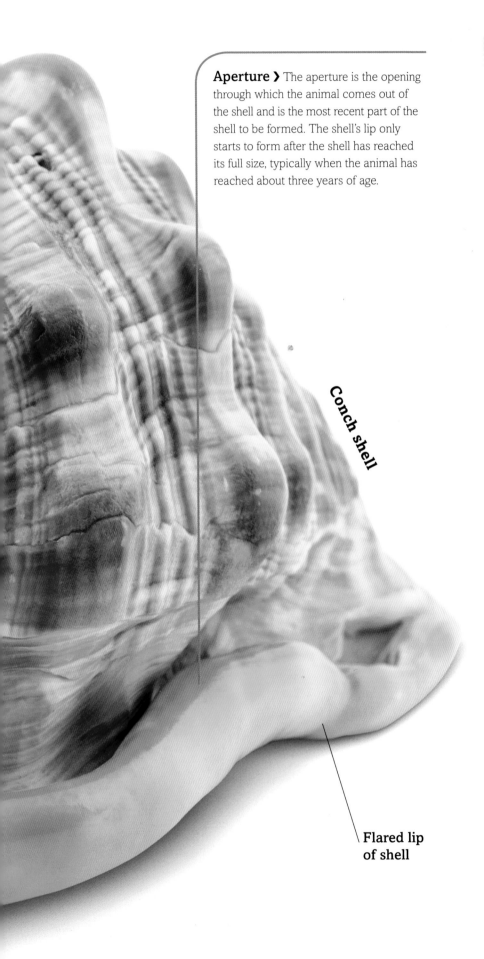

Aperture ❯ The aperture is the opening through which the animal comes out of the shell and is the most recent part of the shell to be formed. The shell's lip only starts to form after the shell has reached its full size, typically when the animal has reached about three years of age.

Conch shell

Flared lip
of shell

Types of shell

Bivalves
• Have two, hinged shells, known as valves. They feed by siphoning water through the shell.

Gastropods
• Live inside a single shell. Most scrape up their food with a tough tongue, called a radula.

Cephalopods
• Typically fast-moving. Only a few live in a single coiled shell; most lack an external shell.

Tusk shells
• Live inside a curved, tube-like shell that is open at both ends. They probe for food in the sea mud.

Chitons
• Have flat shells made up of eight plates. They feed on algae living on rocks.

LIVING MOLLUSCS

Gastropods. Include snails and slugs of all kinds and all sizes, from microscopic to large. They can be found in the sea (right), in freshwater, and also on land.

Bivalves. Include clams, oysters, cockles, mussels, scallops (right), and numerous other families. They live mostly in saltwater, but a number can be found in freshwater.

Tuns, winkles, and relatives

Lesser girdled triton

Tall spire

Pattern of **dark spots** along the opening

Atlantic distorsio

Shells normally have six to seven whorls

Channelled tun

Distinctive **whorl** has deep channel

Spiral of grooves surrounds the opening

Graceful fig shell

Spiral of zigzag lines with red band in between

Zigzag nerite

Deep groove is paler than the rest of the shell

Some larger species of **tun** capture fish and **swallow** them whole.

External pattern visible on the inside of large aperture

Spotted tun

Tuns are carnivorous sea snails, found at all depths. Their name comes from an old term for wine casks. Many have barrel-shaped shells. Winkles – also called periwinkles – are smaller creatures that live along the coastline.

Tuns live in tropical seas and spend the day buried in sandy sea beds, coming out at night to feed mainly on sea cucumbers. Their shells have a typically rounded shape, like the **channelled tun**, which has a body that is wider than it is tall and a very small spire. Tritons, such

Bleeding tooth shell

Wide zigzag *markings cover shell*

Sunburst carrier

Long spines *stick out of the whorls*

Shell *can be up to 33.7 cm (13 in) in length*

Shell *has rows of blunt prickles*

Crowned prickly winkle

Fine ridges *run around shell*

Common periwinkle

Giant frog shell

Moon shell

Surface *of shell is smooth*

Tighter spirals *towards the top*

West Indian worm shell

Tower screw shell

Common nutmeg shell

Shell *has at least 30 turns*

Rounded edges *on the lip of the opening*

Deep-set ridges *run down the shell*

as the **lesser girdled triton**, which lives in the same warm seas, have a taller spire than tuns. The **tower screw shell** has an even taller spire. These tropical snails filter food from the water, an unusual habit for a sea snail. Others have different feeding methods, such as the **common**

periwinkle, which grazes on algae growing on rocks. It is one of the most common snail shells found on the coasts of the north-eastern Atlantic. Tuns' shells also have large openings, or apertures, such as on the **spotted tun**, where the snail's foot pokes out.

Conchs and cowries

Spines stick out from lip

Longest spines are found at top of shell

Sharp spikes surround spire

West Indian fighting conch

Common spider conch

Dog conch

Thick outer lip sticks out from aperture

Violet spider conch

Conchs **graze** on delicate **algae** using a long, thin **snout**.

Long siphon

Silver conch

Broad Pacific conch

Rows of heavy knobs on each whorl

Conchs and cowries are highly prized shells that are collected to make jewellery and ornaments. Conchs are important in both Hinduism and Buddhism. Like most snail shells, conchs with left-handed (anti-clockwise) shells are the rarest.

Conchs are big sea snails that have a sturdy spiral above a large body section. The shape of the **pink conch** is typical of the main group of conchs, known as the strombs. Strombs have a wide, flaring lip that sticks out to the side of the shell aperture. Spider conchs, like the **common spider**

Huge pinkish lip *shows this is an older shell*

Tall, spiralled spire *above smooth body*

Martin's tibia

Powis's tibia

Shinbone tibia

Queen conch

Five strong spines *protect the aperture*

Siphon canal, *through which mollusc tastes water*

Dark, thick rim *surrounds rounded shell*

Golden cowrie

Humpback cowrie

White dots *cover rounded, brown shell*

Lamarck's cowrie

Smooth shell *is orange-gold on top*

Shell *has smooth exterior*

Shuttle volva

Tiger cowrie

Outer lip *sweeps up and over short spire*

Orange stripe *runs from top to bottom*

COLOSSAL CONCH

35.2 cm (13.9 in) long

Queen conch

30 cm (11.8 in) long

Ruler

Monster sea snail
The queen conch is found on the western shore of the Atlantic Ocean, from Brazil to the Caribbean. A big shell has up to 11 whorls and takes around 7 years to grow.

conch and **violet spider conch**, do not have this feature. Instead, the lip is divided into extensions that look like a spider's legs. The **shinbone tibia** belongs to a group of smaller, narrower conchs. The lower part of the shell has a fluted tube into which the snail's siphon (water tube) fits. Cowrie shells are smooth, easy to polish, and have a wide range of patterns, from the spots of the **tiger cowrie** to the rich colours of the **golden cowrie**. The cowrie's whirling spire disappears into the shell as it grows. All cowries have toothed ridges along the opening.

UNUSUAL MOVER
The queen conch is one of the largest marine snails. It lives in the shallow, tropical waters of the western Atlantic coasts of North and Central America and throughout the Caribbean Sea. It has been highly prized by humans for centuries, both as a source of food and for its highly distinctive shell, which typically reaches 15–31 cm (5.9–12.2 in) in length.

After hatching, a queen conch starts its life as a tiny larva, floating in the open ocean and feeding on minute phytoplankton. After 18 to 40 days, it settles into the sand, where it remains buried for the first year of its life, slowly changing into the adult form. Queen conchs reach sexual maturity at three to four years of age, and will typically live for around seven years. They are unusual among sea snails for the way in which they move. They dig the flap that covers the opening of their shell (called the operculum) into the sand, and extend their foot to throw themselves forwards – a little like a pole-vaulter. This shell-thrusting motion is called "leaping", and helps the conch escape danger more quickly.

Augers, cones, and turrids

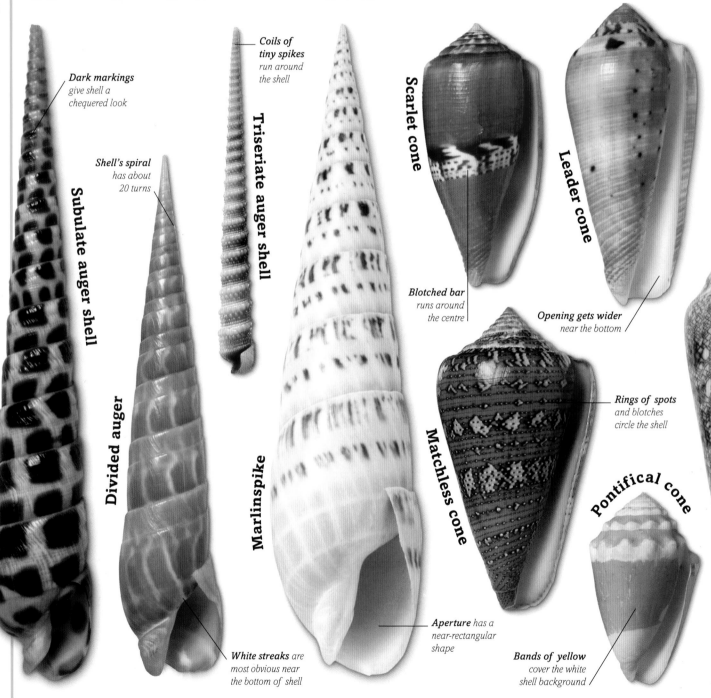

Dark markings
give shell a
chequered look

Shell's spiral
has about
20 turns

Subulate auger shell

Divided auger

Coils of
tiny spikes
run around
the shell

Triseriate auger shell

Marlinspike

White streaks are
most obvious near
the bottom of shell

Scarlet cone

Blotched bar
runs around
the centre

Leader cone

Opening gets wider
near the bottom

Matchless cone

Rings of spots
and blotches
circle the shell

Aperture has a
near-rectangular
shape

Pontifical cone

Bands of yellow
cover the white
shell background

This group of shells are all pointed and cone shaped, but they all share another, much more deadly, characteristic. They are carnivorous sea snails that have specialised mouthparts for pumping venom into prey.

An "auger" is used to describe a small hand drill that is used to bore holes in wood or the ground. Auger shells look like drill bits, and, traditionally, the sharp **marlinspike** shell is used in Asia for that very purpose, for gouging out holes. The **subulate auger** is even sharper, but it lives in

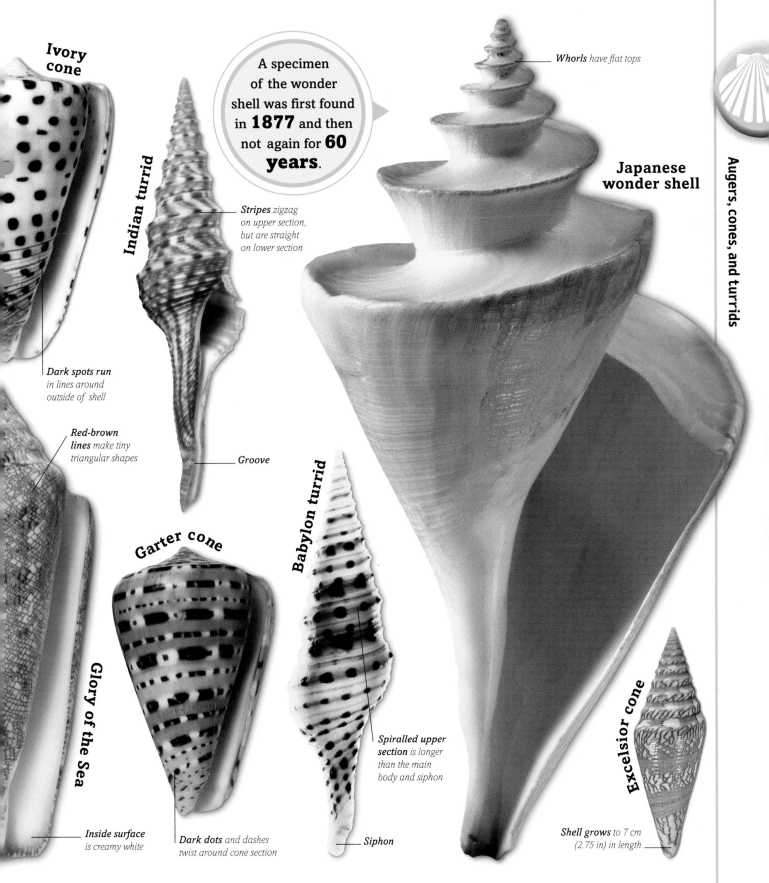

Ivory cone

Indian turrid

A specimen of the wonder shell was first found in **1877** and then not again for **60 years**.

Stripes zigzag on upper section, but are straight on lower section

Dark spots run in lines around outside of shell

Red-brown lines make tiny triangular shapes

Groove

Whorls have flat tops

Japanese wonder shell

Garter cone

Babylon turrid

Glory of the Sea

Spiralled upper section is longer than the main body and siphon

Excelsior cone

Inside surface is creamy white

Dark dots and dashes twist around cone section

Siphon

Shell grows to 7 cm (2.75 in) in length

deep water and so is harder to collect. Pointed turrid shells, such as the **Babylon turrid**, are much more common. They make up the largest family of deep-sea snails, with 4,000 varieties, and most, like the **Indian turrid**, are covered in bumps and nodules. Cone shells are highly varied and are often named after their pattern. For example, the rich, creamy colours of the **pontifical cone** look like the robes worn by the Pope. Cone shells live in shallow, tropical seas and harpoon their prey with fast-acting venom that is powerful enough to kill a human.

Whelks and relatives

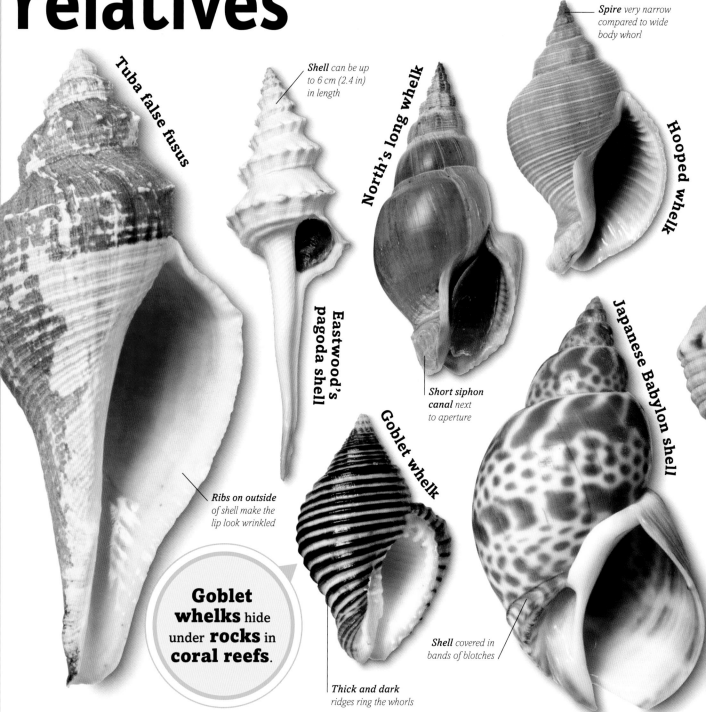

Tuba false fusus

Shell can be up to 6 cm (2.4 in) in length

North's long whelk

Spire very narrow compared to wide body whorl

Hooped whelk

Eastwood's pagoda shell

Short siphon canal next to aperture

Japanese Babylon shell

Goblet whelk

Ribs on outside of shell make the lip look wrinkled

Goblet whelks hide under **rocks** in **coral reefs**.

Shell covered in bands of blotches

Thick and dark ridges ring the whorls

Whelks and whelk-allies are common in cold, rough, coastal seas, but some are tropical or live at greater depths. They are carnivores or scavengers and have excellent sensors for "tasting" the presence of food.

The name "whelk" is applied to many kinds of sea snail – it comes from the words "whirl" and "whorl". The **hooped whelk** belongs to a large group of snails called the neptunes, which can be found all around the world's coasts. The **Eastwood's pagoda shell** comes from

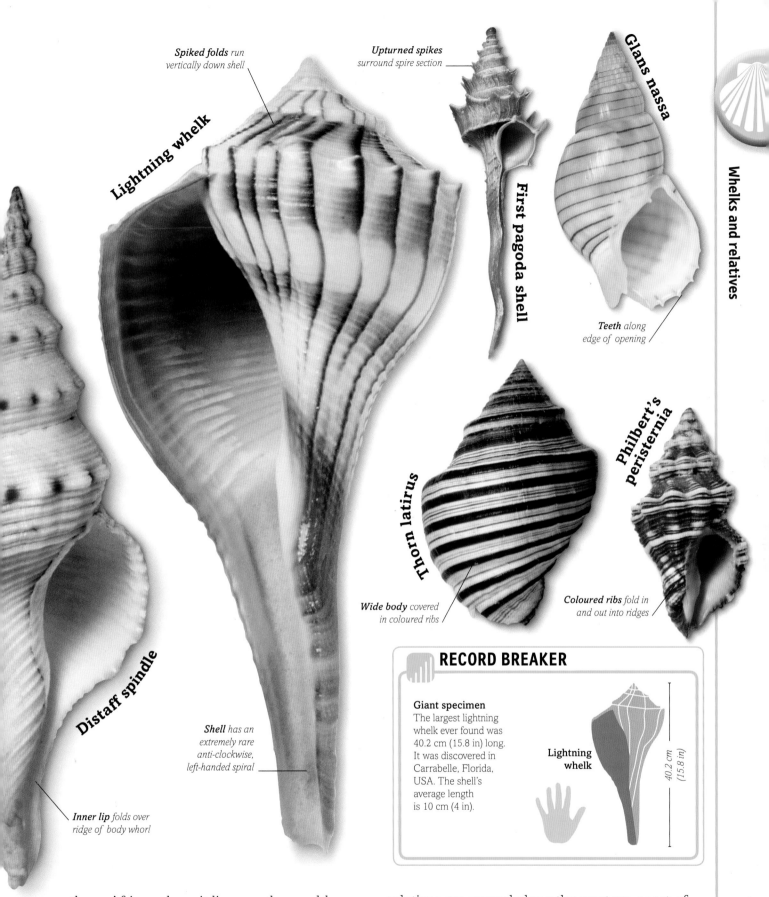

Lightning whelk

Spiked folds run vertically down shell

Upturned spikes surround spire section

First pagoda shell

Glans nassa

Teeth along edge of opening

Thorn latirus

Wide body covered in coloured ribs

Philbert's peristernia

Coloured ribs fold in and out into ridges

Distaff spindle

Shell has an extremely rare anti-clockwise, left-handed spiral

Inner lip folds over ridge of body whorl

RECORD BREAKER

Giant specimen
The largest lightning whelk ever found was 40.2 cm (15.8 in) long. It was discovered in Carrabelle, Florida, USA. The shell's average length is 10 cm (4 in).

Lightning whelk

40.2 cm (15.8 in)

southern Africa, where it lives on the muddy sea bed. The **distaff spindle** has a similar shape to the pagoda shells and is characterized by the brown-orange striped markings on its spindle. The **lightning whelk** is found along the coast of Florida and eastern North America, and its relatives are spread along the western coast of the Atlantic. The **glans nassa** is one of the nassa mud snails from Southeast Asia. The **thorn latirus** and **Philbert's peristernia** are both members of a large group of small, carnivorous snails that live worldwide.

Murexes and relatives

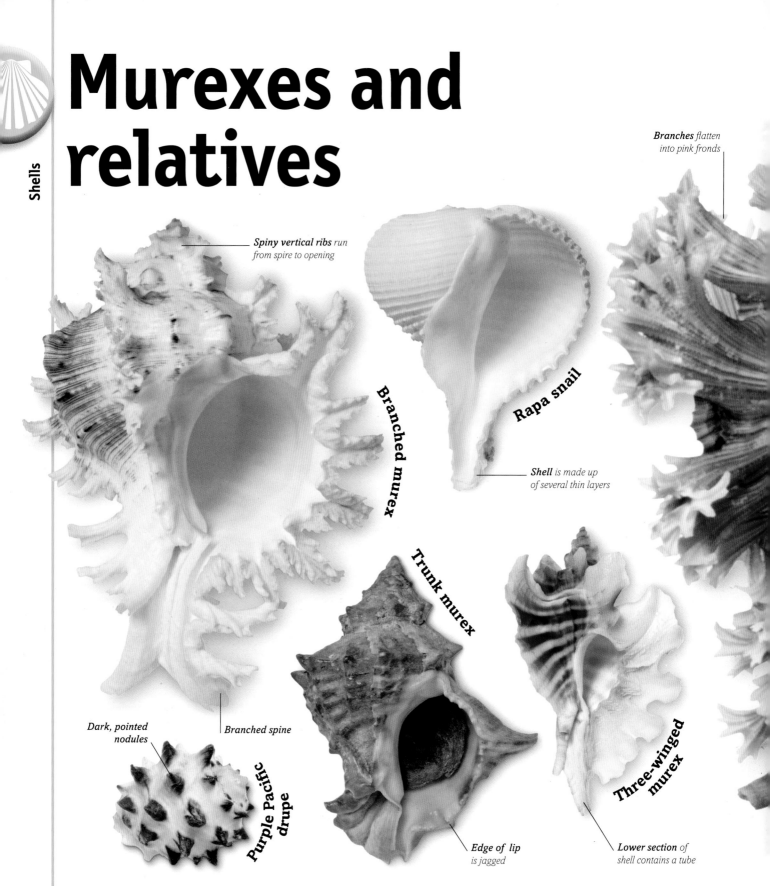

Branches flatten into pink fronds

Spiny vertical ribs run from spire to opening

Branched murex

Rapa snail

Shell is made up of several thin layers

Trunk murex

Dark, pointed nodules

Branched spine

Purple Pacific drupe

Three-winged murex

Edge of lip is jagged

Lower section of shell contains a tube

The murexes are a highly varied group of snails with amazingly complex shells. The spirals of the shells are hard to see among all the frills, spines, and plates that stick out in all directions. Murexes are predators that live in warm, shallow seas.

Murex snails were highly prized in the ancient world, as their shells were ground down to make a purple dye the wealthiest Romans used to colour their clothes. The **trunk murex** was collected for the same reason. The beautiful pink colour of the **rose branch murex** makes

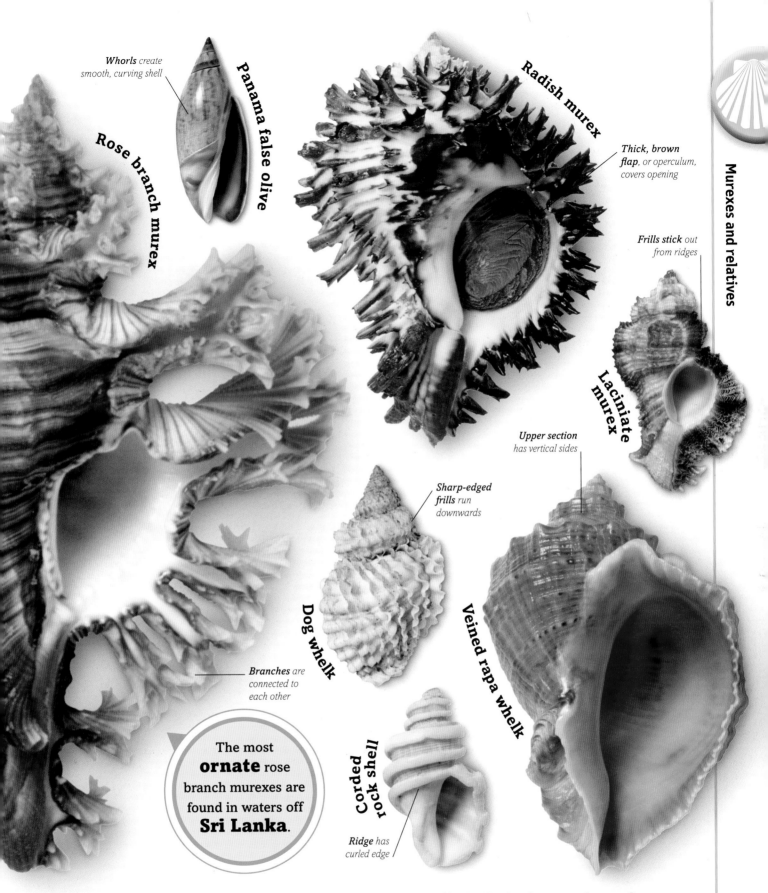

Panama false olive

Whorls create smooth, curving shell

Rose branch murex

Radish murex

Thick, brown flap, or operculum, covers opening

Frills stick out from ridges

Laciniate murex

Upper section has vertical sides

Sharp-edged frills run downwards

Dog whelk

Veined rapa whelk

Branches are connected to each other

The most **ornate** rose branch murexes are found in waters off **Sri Lanka**.

Corded rock shell

Ridge has curled edge

it highly valued by shell collectors. However, many are given extra colours by unscrupulous traders. The **purple Pacific drupe** shares its name with a group of fruits that have a stone in the middle – the shell looks like a colourful fruit stone. Rock shells, like the **corded rock shell**,

have shells similar in shape to those of murexes. However, the **dog whelk** is only frilled when it lives in sheltered waters; in rough conditions it is smooth. The **veined rapa whelk** grinds through the shells of other molluscs and can inflict huge damage on oyster beds.

169

Other snails

Rumphius' slit shell

Long slit *runs through body whorl*

Long ribbed limpet

Shell *has unique array of radiating ridges*

Turban shells are named from *Turbo*, Latin for **spinning top**.

Clear sundial

Two striped ribs *run around base of shell*

Silver mouth turban

Mother of pearl *appears through patches of shell covering*

South African turban

Painted lady

Thick ribs *visible on inside of shell*

Rippled *light and dark bands run vertically down smooth shell*

Turban shells and limpets are among the most primitive of the sea snails. Like almost all other sea snails, they use gills to breathe in water. Land snails and most freshwater snails have lungs to breathe air.

Limpets cling firmly to rocks, and the shell of the **long ribbed limpet** is shaped to fit a particular space. When the tide goes out and the shell is exposed to the air, the limpet pulls its shell down to seal in any water underneath – this prevents the animal from drying out and

Spines *at right angles to whorl*

Triumphant star turban

Bridled bolma

Curved spines curl downwards

Eloise shell

Bordered horn and chevron shapes on white background

Rows of tooth-shaped pointed scales

Sunburst star turban

Dots and dashes run around the shell

Coiled shell of this freshwater species resembles ram's horn

Ram's horn snail

Chequered top

Newly hatched snail

Brown garden snail

Lining has iridescent colour

Donkey's ear abalone

Brown stripes spiral out from centre of shell of this land snail

Lister's keyhole limpet

Shell has small hole at top called the "keyhole"

means it can carry on breathing. When underwater, **Lister's keyhole limpet** pumps a flow of water into its shell and squirts it out of the top through an opening called the "keyhole". **Rumphius' slit shell** does something similar, by pumping out water through the slit in the side of its shell. The **chequered top** looks similar to the slit shell, but lacks the slit. It is named after the way it resembles an upside-down spinning top. The **triumphant star turban** has several spikes sticking out of the side.

FLOATING THE WAVES
While most snails slither around on their single, flexible foot, the bubble raft snail takes a ride on the ocean's currents, floating under a raft of bubbles. The snail is a predator that attacks other floating creatures, most often the Portuguese man o' war, which is a relative of the jellyfish. It is a hit-and-miss lifestyle, however; the snail cannot swim and can only go where the ocean takes it.

To make its raft, the bubble raft snail traps bubbles of air in mucus, which hardens to keep it secure. The resulting air-filled float sticks to the snail's foot and its thin, lightweight shell ensures it stays afloat. The snail lives its life upside down, with the spire of its shell pointing towards the ocean floor. It protects itself through camouflage on its shell, using a trick known as "countershading". The spire and whorls of its shell are pale in colour, while the region around the opening is a deep blue-purple. This means that, seen from above, the blue shell is difficult to spot among the dark ocean water; from below, the shell's pale colours blend in with the sunbeams shining down.

Clams, cockles, and relatives

Lazarus jewel box

Philippine watering pot

Sand and shell *fragments stuck to tube shell*

Cradle donax

Horizontal lines are growth rings

Common European cockle

Front edge is smooth and rounded

Shell covered in leaflike plates

Hinge

Giant cockles can reach **12.7 cm (5 in)** in length.

Toothed edge

Giant cockle shell

Clams and cockles are bivalves, molluscs that have two shells connected by a hinge. Similar seashells include tellins and surf shells. These animals are mostly filter feeders; they draw water into the shell and filter out any particles of food.

Clams and cockles tend to have more symmetrical shells than other bivalves. An excellent example is the **ox-heart clam**, which displays almost complete symmetry, as does the **true heart cockle**. The **angel wing**, so-named because its white shell is shaped like the

Swan mussel

Royal comb venus

Deep ridges *end in long spines poking backwards*

Camp pitar venus

Narrow green, yellow, and black *stripes cover the shell surface in this freshwater species*

Tent-shaped, *or hieroglyphic, markings*

True heart cockle

Blood-stained sanguin

Pink-spotted *markings on shell. They can also be yellow, violet, and white.*

Giant razor shell

Pinkish shell *becomes darker around the hinge*

Shell *is almost rectangular in shape*

Ridges *inside shell as well as outside*

Sunset siliqua

Australian brooch clam

Pale stripes *on shell*

Clear ridges *on outside of shell*

Angel wing

Ox-heart clam

Stripes *cover shell's surface*

Striped tellin

Shell *grows to about 10 cm (4 in) in length*

MIGHTY MOLLUSC

|← 1.37 m (4.5 ft) →| |← 1.7 m (5.5 ft) →|

Giant clam   Diver

Giant of the sea bed
Giant clams are the largest of the shelled molluscs. They can reach 1.37 m (4.5 ft) in length and can live for more than 100 years.

feathered wings of an angel, is an exception, being much longer on one side than the other. **The giant razor** shell is named after the sharp, straight edge of its valves. It is mostly found buried in the sand near the low-water line. The **giant cockle** also prefers sandy habitats, although it lives at greater depths. The **striped tellin** lives in the sea bed, using siphons several times longer than its shell to connect to the water above. The venus clams, such as the **royal comb venus** and **camp pitar venus**, are named after the Roman goddess of love.

SUPER-SIZED SHELL
The largest shellfish of all, the giant clam lives a quiet life among the corals, sponges, and seaweeds of a tropical reef. It can outlive most of its neighbours, and, on average, lives for 100 years. During that time, the outside of the clam's shell becomes encrusted with barnacles and many other hangers-on; other life forms make a home inside this ocean giant's shell.

The giant clam's mighty valves close tightly enough to grip anything trapped between them, including a human arm. However, the mollusc only clams up when threatened, and it closes so slowly that no diver would be caught unaware. During the day, the clam has its shell fully open, filtering food from the water. However, the clam gets most of its food from microscopic algae that live inside its body tissues. In return for a safe place to live, the algae share the sugars they produce naturally with their host. This sharing arrangement, known as " mutualistic symbiosis", means the clam is nourished by extra food and can grow into a giant.

Oysters, scallops, and relatives

European bittersweet

Tooth-shaped markings

Serrated edge
along inside of shell

Rough scales
stick out from ribs on shell

Pacific file shell

Pacific thorny oyster

Thick spines
run in lines down the shell

Noah's ark

Thorny oysters were **traded** as **ornaments** as early as **4500** BCE.

Irregular stripes
extend around shell

Toga awning clam

Outer shell covering extends in teeth at the front

Valves connected at base of shell

Oysters come in many different types, but all are famed for their ability to produce pearls. Scallops' shells have rounded valves, earlike projections at the hinge, and are probably the most familiar seashell shape of all.

The shape of the shell is not the only difference between oysters and scallops; they tend to live in different habitats, too. The **Pacific thorny oyster** and **cock's comb oyster**, for example, become fastened to a rocky surface at an early stage in their development and do not move.

Triangular fold

Shell opens when scallop is underwater for feeding

Living mollusc inside shell

Great scallop

One ear bigger than the other

Tiny bumps on inside edges

Cock's comb oyster

Purple-brown colour inside shell

Austral scallop

Nine main ribs with many tiny riblets

Lion's paw

Queen scallop

— *Umbone*

Royal cloak scallop

European jingle shell

Shell moulded to shape of sea floor

Right valve less curved than left valve

In contrast, the **austral scallop**, **lion's paw**, and **queen scallop** keep on the move for most of their lives. They open then close their valves rapidly to create a jet of water that propels them along in spurts or even enables them to swim in open water. The **great scallop** is too large to move that much and spends most of its life lying on the sandy sea bed. The **Pacific file shell** is also able to swim by clapping its valves together. It gets its name from the sawlike edge of its valves and the rough surface of its shell.

Strange shells

Spikes protect the sea floor animal

Rock minerals have replaced the hard body parts

Heart urchin fossil

Hermit crab in a shell

Rear end

Shell left by dead whelk

Sea urchin

Bony plates under skin add protection

Girdle surrounds eight shells

Marbled chiton

Coarse spines surround plates

Blue-green underside

Fuzzy chiton

LARGEST CHITON

33 cm (13 in)

Giant of the family
The northern Pacific gumboot chiton is the largest chiton in the world. It is 33 cm (13 in) long and weighs 2 kg (4.4 lb).

Most molluscs are gastropods (such as snails and slugs) or bivalves (including the clams and oysters). However, there are other kinds of molluscs that make different kinds of shells, and other kinds of shellfish that are not molluscs at all.

The **marbled chiton** is an example of a small group of molluscs. Instead of having one shell like the gastropods, or two like the bivalves, these animals have eight valves that overlap each other to make a flexible coat of armour. Chitons are grazers that eat the microbes that grow on rocks.

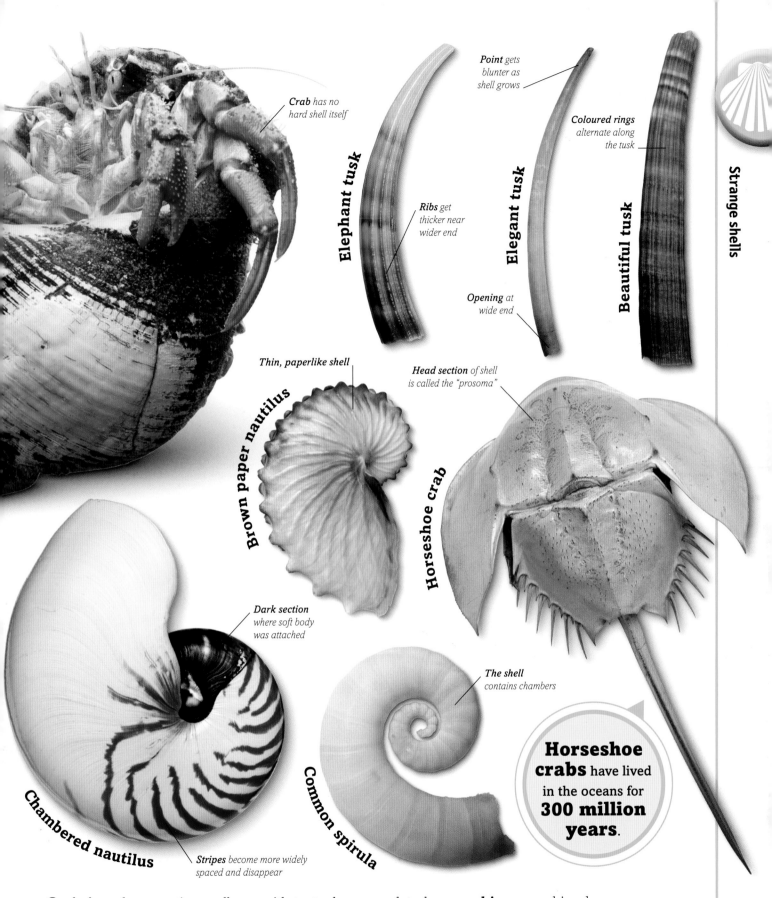

Crab has no hard shell itself

Elephant tusk

Point gets blunter as shell grows

Ribs get thicker near wider end

Opening at wide end

Elegant tusk

Coloured rings alternate along the tusk

Beautiful tusk

Strange shells

Thin, paperlike shell

Brown paper nautilus

Head section of shell is called the "prosoma"

Horseshoe crab

Dark section where soft body was attached

The shell contains chambers

Chambered nautilus

Stripes become more widely spaced and disappear

Common spirula

Horseshoe crabs have lived in the oceans for **300 million years**.

Cephalopods are active molluscs with tentacles. They include soft, shell-less octopuses, as well as squids and cuttlefish with internal shells. Only a few cephalopods – **nautilus** and **spirula** – have external shells. **Elephant tusk** and other sand-burrowing **tusk shells** are also molluscs. Bony-plated **sea urchins** are echinoderms – a group that includes starfish. **Horseshoe crabs** are joint-legged arthropods, more closely related to spiders and scorpions. True crabs are arthropods too – including **hermit crabs** that commandeer discarded shells of dead snails for protection.

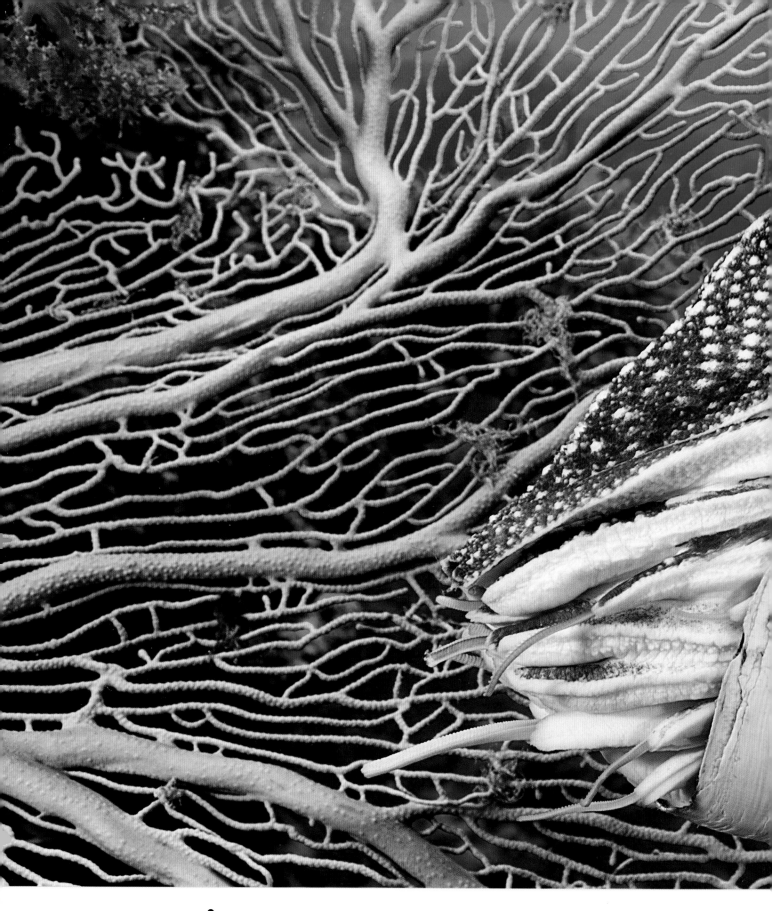

NATURE'S SUBMARINE

The chambered nautilus is a relative of squids and octopuses. Together, they make up a group of molluscs called cephalopods. Like other cephalopods, the nautilus swims freely, has tentacles for grabbing prey, and a horny beak for biting through shells. However, unlike its relatives, the chambered nautilus lives inside a shell.

The chambered nautilus is the closest thing the natural world has to a submarine. The spiral shell is made up of many chambers, and the nautilus lives in the largest one. When it outgrows that chamber, it adds on a bigger one, sealing off the unwanted smaller chamber behind it. A tube runs through all the chambers and allows the nautilus to control how much water is in each sealed chamber. Adding water makes it sink; taking it out makes the animal float up. Like all cephalopods, the nautilus moves using jet power, squirting a jet of water out of the shell. This means the nautilus moves shell-first. It has about 90 tentacles that grip and hold of prey thanks to ridges on their surface.

Glossary

Accessory minerals
A minor mineral that is present in small amounts in a rock.

Achondrite
A stony meteorite that does not contain chondrules (round crystalline balls).

Asteroid
A chunk of rock, smaller than a planet, which orbits the Sun.

Batholith
A very large igneous intrusion of molten magma underground.

Bedrock
The solid rock that lies under soil and sediments.

Botryoidal
A mineral habit that resembles a bunch of grapes.

Breccia
A sedimentary rock made up of angular fragments.

Cabochon
A gemstone that is polished but not faceted (flat faces cut in it).

Calcareous
A rock that contains a significant amount of calcium carbonate mineral, or is chalky.

Canyon
A deep, steep-sided valley, typically cut by a river.

Carat
The standard measure of weight for precious stones and metals. A carat is equal to 0.2 g (0.007 oz).

Chalcedony
A microcrystalline type of quartz. The most common is agate, but it can occur in different forms, including onyx.

Chondrite
A stony meteorite containing tiny spherical chondrules.

Cleavage
The characteristic way a mineral or rock breaks along a certain plane, or in a certain direction.

Coccolith
A microscopic rounded platelet made of the mineral calcium carbonate, which once formed a part of the spherical shells of a tiny planktonic animal.

Concretion
A hard and compact rocky lump formed when mineral cement is deposited in the spaces between sedimentary particles. Often rounded or oval, they are found in shale and clay beds, as well as soils.

Crystal
A naturally occurring solid substance whose atoms are arranged in a regular 3-D pattern.

Crystal system
The systems into which crystals are grouped based on their symmetry. There are six crystal systems: cubic, monoclinic, triclinic, trigonal/ hexagonal, orthorhombic, and tetragonal.

Dendritic
A crystal habit that looks like branching "fingers".

Dodecahedral
A crystal or mineral with a dodecahedron shape – a 3-D form with 12 faces.

Element
A chemical substance that cannot be broken down further.

Erosion
Gradual wear and transport of the solid surface of Earth by wind, water, and ice. It grinds down rocks and shapes the land.

Evaporite
A natural salt mineral formed from residues left behind when briny water has evaporated.

Extinct
A group of organisms (animals, plants, fungi, or microorganisms) that has no living members and is no longer in existence. Many fossils, such as dinosaurs and trilobites, belong to extinct groups.

Extrusive rock
An igneous rock that formed from magma that solidified above ground.

Face
An external flat surface on a rough crystal.

Facet
A flat face cut into a gemstone. A cut stone is called faceted.

Fault
An extended fracture or weakness in rock – often a flat plane – along which rock masses move. A fault line is where a fault appears.

Fibrous
A mineral habit composed of thin fibres.

Fluorescence
The optical effect whereby a mineral appears to glow in ultraviolet (UV) light. It often glows a different colour under UV light than it does in ordinary light.

Fossil
A trace of past life that has been preserved in a rock or mineral such as amber. Fossils include bones, shells, skin impressions, footprints, dung, wood, leaves, and pollen.

Fossiliferous
A rock containing fossils.

Fracture
The distinctive way in which a mineral breaks.

Gemstone
A beautiful, high-quality, hard mineral, which is valued for its colour and rarity. Gems usually have a near-perfect, or unique, crystal shape.

Geode
A cavity in a rock that has been filled, or partially filled, with crystals. It is sometimes called a "thunder egg".

Identifying minerals

There are many ways to identify a mineral, including observing its colour and shape, and how it looks when it reflects light. The hardness of a mineral can be measured by how easily it scratches.

COLOUR

Many minerals have characteristic colours that make them instantly recognizable. Others, such as fluorite, come in a range of tones, which are due to different impurities in the crystals.

Purple fluorite   **Green fluorite**

LUSTRE

Lustre is the way a mineral reflects light. There are a number of terms to describe this, from waxy to metallic, earthy, and vitreous (glassy).

Galena:
metallic lustre

Quartz:
vitreous lustre

SPECIFIC GRAVITY

A mineral's specific gravity is a measure of its density. This is calculated by weighing a crystal and comparing it to the mass of an equal volume of water. This requires specialist equipment.

Jasper: 2.7

STREAK

A mineral may not always appear the same colour. It may have been altered by weathering, for example. So geologists carry a hard ceramic scratch plate and test a mineral's "streak", which does not vary.

Orpiment

Cinnabar

FRACTURE

Minerals also crack and splinter in other directions to their cleavage. The way they do this is often typical of a mineral.

Obsidian: shell-like fracture

TRANSPARENCY

If light can pass through a mineral, it is called translucent. If a mineral is opaque, no light can pass through it. Transparent minerals are clear and see-through.

Calcite is
transparent

CLEAVAGE

Most crystals have planes of weakness along which they will break, known as their cleavage. Because crystal structures are regular and repeating, they break again and again along characteristic angles.

Topaz cleaves, or
breaks, into a prism-
shaped crystal

HARDNESS

One of the easiest tests is to find a mineral's hardness. This is measured on Mohs' scale – a relative scale, from 1–10, tested by scratching the mineral – or by using it to scratch something else.

Talc: 1 – can be cut
with fingernail

Diamond: 10 –
can cut glass

HABIT

The outward appearance of a crystal is called its habit. A mineral's habit depends on the pattern that its crystals form as they grow. If there is no clear shape, it is called "massive".

Vivanite:
needlelike

Gypsum:
bladed

Groundmass
The compact, fine-grained mineral material in which larger crystals or grains are embedded.

Habit
The general appearance and shape of a mineral. A mineral's habit can be affected by its crystal system and the conditions under which it grew.

Ice cap
A thick covering of ice over an area of land. Larger ice caps more than 50,000 sq km (19,305 sq miles) are usually called ice sheets.

Igneous rock
A rock formed when molten lava or magma solidifies on or below Earth's surface.

Impurity
An atom or chemical compound incorporated into a mineral's crystal structure that is not an essential part of its makeup. It often affects the colour of minerals and gems.

Inclusion
Any material that gets trapped inside a crystal during its formation.

Ingot
A solid block of metal, typically rectangular in shape.

Intrusive rock
An igneous rock that forms when magma solidifies below the surface.

Invertebrate
An animal with no backbone, such as worms and arthropods.

Lava
Magma that has flowed onto Earth's surface through a volcanic opening.

Lustre
The way in which light reflects off the surface of a mineral.

Magma
Molten rock found deep inside Earth. Magma collects in a magma chamber to feed a volcano.

Mantle
The layer of the planet that lies between the core and the crust. It contains over 80 per cent of Earth's total volume, and consists of hot, dense rocks.

Matrix
Also known as groundmass, the matrix of a rock is the fine-grained mass in which larger grains or crystals are embedded.

Metamorphic rock
A rock that has been transformed within Earth by heat or pressure, or both.

Meteor
A meteoroid (rock and dust debris in space) that burns up as it travels through Earth's atmosphere, appearing as a bright streak, or "shooting star", in the night sky.

Meteorite
A rock or dusty debris from outer space that reaches the surface of Earth.

Microcrystalline
A mineral habit that is made up of microscopic crystals.

Mineral
A naturally occurring solid that has specific characteristics, such as a particular chemical composition and crystal shape.

Native element
A chemical element found in nature in its pure form.

Nodule
A hard, rounded, stony lump found in sedimentary rock. It is typically made from calcite, silica, pyrite, or gypsum.

Nugget
A small lump of a precious metal found in its native state.

Octahedral
A crystal or mineral that has an octagon shape – a solid 3-D form with eight faces.

Opaque
A substance that does not let light pass through it.

Ore
A rock or mineral from which a metal can be extracted.

Organic
Relating to living things.

Pearly
A mineral lustre with a soft sheen, like a pearl.

Petrification
The process by which a living thing turns to stone fossil in a rock.

Pigment
A coloured substance that is powdered and mixed to make paint.

Pisolitic
A rock texture formed of pea-sized balls.

Placer deposit
A deposit of sand or gravel on a river bed or lake bed, with particles of valuable minerals.

Plateau
An area of high-level ground.

Polymorph
A mineral with an identical chemical composition but a different structure.

Porphyritic
A rock texture made of larger crystals embedded in a fine-grained groundmass. Typical of volcanic rocks.

Prism
A solid 3-D form whose two end faces are the same shape, equal size, and parallel to one another.

Prismatic
Crystals with a uniform cross-section, having parallel long sides.

Recrystallization
The process by which secondary minerals grow; changes in a rock when heat or pressure cause minerals to regrow.

Rock
A solid mixture of minerals. There are three types: igneous, metamorphic, and sedimentary.

Secondary mineral
A mineral that replaces another as a result of weathering or other alteration process.

Sediment
Particles of rock, mineral, or organic matter that are carried by wind, water, and ice.

Sedimentary rock
A rock formed from sediments that have been cemented together by weathering or burial.

Shield volcano
A broad volcano with gently sloping sides that produces swift-flowing basalt lavas.

Smelting
The chemical process of extracting metal from its mineral ores.

Striation
A prominent groove in a rock or mineral, usually all in the same direction.

Tectonic plate
One of the huge, rocky slabs into which the outer layer of our planet is broken. Heat within Earth drives tectonic plates across the surface. Volcanoes and earthquakes happen where these plates bump and crash into each other.

Translucent
A substance that allows light to pass though it.

Twinning
Crystals that share a common face or edge.

Volcanic bomb
A large lump of lava that is ejected into the air from a volcano.

Volcano
The site of an eruption of lava and hot gases from within the Earth. Magma follows a central passage to reach the surface and erupts as lava.

Weathering
The slow breakdown of rock by long exposure to the weather, including moisture, frost, and chemical rainwater.

Wingspan
The distance from wingtip to wingtip, when the wings are fully outstretched.

Index

A-C

Wavellite

D–G

H–L

Logan Sapphire

Precious opal

Celestine

ACKNOWLEDGEMENTS

The publisher would like to thank the following people for their help with making the book: Sonam Mathur, Ateendriya Gupta, Daisy, Rupa Rao, Sreshtha Bhattacharya, and Virien Chopra for editorial assistance; Heena Sharma, Nidhi Rastogi, and Sanjay Chauhan for design assistance; Syed Md Farhan and Nand Kishore Acharya for DTP assistance; Kealy Wilson and Ellen Nanney from the Smithsonian Institution; Hazel Beynon for proofreading; and Helen Peters for indexing. Additional text by Tom Jackson.

The publisher would like to thank the following for their kind permission to reproduce their photographs:

(Key: a-above; b-below/bottom; c-centre; f-far; l-left; r-right; t-top)

1 Corbis: Walter Geiersperger (c). **4 Alamy Images:** PjrStudio (cr). **5 Dorling Kindersley:** Senckenberg Gesellschaft Fuer Naturforschung (cr). **6 Corbis:** Charles O'Rear (bl). **Dorling Kindersley:** The Senckenberg Nature Museum, Frankfurt (bc). **National Museum of Natural History, Smithsonian Institution:** Dane A. Penland (tr). **7 Alamy Images:** PjrStudio (bl). **Corbis:** Layne Kennedy (br). **Dorling Kindersley:** The Natural History Museum, London (tc, bc). **Dreamstime.com:** Ingemar Magnusson (br). **8 Science Photo Library:** RICHARD BIZLEY (tl). **12-13 Alamy Images:** Bill Bachman (br). **15 Alamy Images:** keith taylor (br). **Corbis:** Frank Krahmer (crb). **Dreamstime.com:** Glenn Nagel (cr). **16 Alamy Images:** Siim Sepp (bl). **Dorling Kindersley:** The Natural History Museum, London (tl, tc). **16-17 Alamy Images:** PjrStudio (tc). **Dorling Kindersley:** The Oxford University Museum of Natural History (c). **17 123RF.com:** Jirawat Plekhongthu (ca). **Alamy Images:** Siim Sepp (crb). **Dorling Kindersley:** The Natural History Museum, London (cr). **Getty Images:** De Agostini / A. Rizzi (tc). **18 Dorling Kindersley:** The Natural History Museum, London (tl). **Dreamstime.com:** Carolina K. Smith M.d. (cb); Pathompoom Srikudvien (cr). **19 123RF.com:** Wasin Pummarin (ba). **Alamy Images:** World History Archive (tr); Nina Matthews (tl). **iStockphoto.com:** shirhan (tc). **20-21 Dorling Kindersley:** The Oxford University Museum of Natural History (bc). **21 123RF.com:** PaylessImages (tc). **Dorling Kindersley:** The University of Aberdeen (c); The Natural History Museum, London (tl). **Getty Images:** John Cancalosi (c). **22 123RF.com:** Kjetil Dahle (clb/lava). **Corbis:** Leemage (bc); Roger Ressmeyer (cr); Ralph White (bl). **Dorling Kindersley:** The Natural History Museum, London (c). **Dreamstime.com:** Rafal Kubiak (tc). **22-23 Alamy Images:** Buddy Mays (c). **23 Alamy Images:** Simone A. Brandt (tl); Franco Salmoiraghi (tc). **Corbis:** Angelo Hornak (tr). **Dreamstime.com:** Andrea G. Ricordi (br/causeway). **Getty Images:** De Agostini (ca). **Science Photo Library:** NASA (bl). **24-25 Getty Images:** Toshi Sasaki (c). **26-27 Alamy Images:** Siim Sepp (bc). **26 Dorling Kindersley:** The Natural History Museum, London (tr). **Dreamstime.com:** Mitchell Barutha (fcl); Bahrin Diana (cl). **Getty Images:** John Cancalosi (bc). **27 Corbis:** Visuals Unlimited (tc). **Dorling Kindersley:** The Natural History Museum, London (bc). **28 Dorling Kindersley:** The Natural History Museum, London (ca). **Dreamstime.com:** Nastya81 (clb); Cenk Unver (r). **29 Alamy Images:** Nitschkefoto (cra); PjrStudio (crb); picturedimensions (cr). **Dorling Kindersley:** Oxford University Museum of Natural History (ca); The Natural History Museum, London (br). **Getty Images:** Space Images (r). **30 Alamy Images:** geoz (ca). **31 123RF.com:** zelfit (cb). **Alamy Images:** Sabena Jane Blackbird (cl); Manfred Gottschalk (crb). **32 Dreamstime.com:** Javarman (cb). **33 Alamy Images:** John Cancalosi (cr). **34 Alamy Images:** Siim Sepp (cb). **Corbis:** Vittorio Sciosia (clb). **Dreamstime.com:** Srijan Roy Chouhudry (crb); Jimmyconnor07 (tr). **Science Photo Library:** SCIENTIFICA, VISUALS UNLIMITED (cr). **35 Alamy Images:** John Cancalosi (cl); Siim Sepp (c). **Dreamstime.com:** Byelikova (tc); Bambi L. Dingman (cl). **36-37 Corbis:** Imaginechina. **38 Dorling Kindersley:** NASA (tr); The Natural History Museum, London (clb, c). **Science Photo Library:** Larry French (cb). **Science Photo Library:** DR JUERG ALEAN (tl). **38-39 Science Photo Library:** DETLEV VAN RAVENSWAAY (c). **39 Dorling Kindersley:** NASA (cla). **Dreamstime.com:** Cylonphoto (tr). **Press Association Images:** Elmar Buchner (cra). **Science Photo Library:** PETRIE MUSEUM OF EGYPTIAN ARCHAEOLOGY, UCL (c). **40-41 Getty Images:** Frans Lanting (c). **42-43 Corbis:** Darrell Gulin (c). **45 Dorling Kindersley:** The Natural History Museum, London (cla). **46 Dorling Kindersley:** The Natural History Museum, London (cla). **Dreamstime.com:** Omendrive (cl). **47 Dorling Kindersley:** Alan Keohane (tc); The Natural History Museum, London (c). **Dreamstime.com:** Peter Hermes Furian (tl); Pictac (cr); Joools (bc). **48 Corbis:** The Gallery Collection (clb); Charles O'Rear (tl). **Dorling Kindersley:** Colin Keates (tr). **49 Corbis:** Mark Weiss (bl). **Dorling Kindersley:** University of Pennsylvania Museum of Archaeology and Anthropology (cr); Canterbury City Council, Museums and Galleries (cl). **Dreamstime.com:** Andrey Armyagov (crb). **50 123RF.com:** Veerachai Viteeman (tr). **Dorling Kindersley:** The National Music Museum (l); The Natural History Museum, London (c, clb). **51 123RF.com:** foottoo (tl). **Alamy Images:** The Natural History Museum, London (tl). **Dorling Kindersley:** Durham University Oriental Museum (c); The University of Aberdeen (clb). **Dreamstime.com:** Gaurav Masand (cl); Slavapolo (cb). **52 Alamy Images:** ASK Images (crb). **Dorling Kindersley:** The Natural History Museum, London (tl, c, clb, cb). **Dreamstime.com:** Kopitinphoto (tc); Noiral (cl); Marsel307 (cr). **52-53 Dorling Kindersley:** The Oxford University Museum of Natural History (c). **53 Dreamstime.com:** Ingemar Magnusson (cb); Marcovarro (tr). **Getty Images:** Tim Graham (clb). **National Museum of Natural History, Smithsonian Institution:** Chip Clark (tc, cl); Dane A. Penland (cr). **54 Dorling Kindersley:** The Oxford University Museum of Natural History (cr). **54-55 Corbis:** Scientifica (cl). **55 123RF.com:** Aleksandar Kosev (tl). **Alamy Images:** BigJoker (tr). **Corbis:** Arne Hodalic (ca). **Dorling Kindersley:** The University of Aberdeen (cb). **Science Photo Library:** The NATURAL HISTORY MUSEUM (l); JOSE ANTONIO PEÑAS (cra). **56-57 Alamy Images:** Dale O'Dell. **58 Corbis:** Jeff Daly (tr). **60 Corbis:** Mark Schneider (crb). **Dorling Kindersley:** The Natural History Museum, London (crb). **61 Dorling Kindersley:** The Natural History Museum, London (cra). **62 Alamy Images:** World History Archive (cb); Universal Images Group / DeAgostini (cl). **Corbis:** Scientifica / Corbis (clb). **Dorling Kindersley:** The Natural History Museum, London (cra). **63 123RF.**

com: paulrommer (ca). **Alamy Images:** World History Archive (clb); Marvin Dembinsky Photo Associates (cla). **Dorling Kindersley:** The Board of Trustees of the Royal Armouries (t). **Dreamstime.com:** Smallow (cra). **64 123RF.com:** Christopher Howey (cla). **Dreamstime.com:** Epitavi (cra); Anton Starikov (cl). **Science Photo Library:** GUSTOIMAGES (cra). **64-65 Dreamstime.com:** Zbynek Burival (bc). **65 Alamy Images:** Alan Curtis / LGPL (cla). **Corbis:** Harley-Davidson (cra). **Dreamstime.com:** Carlosvelayos (cr); Ingemar Magnusson (tl). **66 Alamy Images:** Pat Behnke (cb). **Dreamstime.com:** Loiren (crb). **67 Alamy Images:** Brian Jackson (crb). **Dorling Kindersley:** The Natural History Museum, London (c). **68 Dorling Kindersley:** The Natural History Museum, London (tl). **69 Alamy Images:** The Natural History Museum, London (ca). **Dorling Kindersley:** The Natural History Museum, London (tl). **Dreamstime.com:** Chinaview (tc). **70 Alamy Images:** John Hyde / Design Pics Inc (cb). **Corbis:** Mike Grandmaison (cl); Roger Ressmeyer (cra). **Dreamstime.com:** Rita Jayaraman (cr). **Getty Images:** Westend61 (tr). **National Geographic Creative:** SISSE BRIMBERG & COTTON COULSON, KEENPRESS (tl). **71 Corbis:** Radius Images (tl); Wayne Lynch / All Canada Photos (c). **Dreamstime.com:** Andrew Buckin / Ka_ru (ca). **Getty Images:** Jonathan & Angela Scott (cb). **Photoshot:** Frans Lanting (clb). **72-73 Corbis:** Tom Bean. **74 Corbis:** Mark Schneider / Visuals Unlimited (cl, c). **75 Corbis:** Phil Degginger (crb). **Corbis:** Mark Schneider / Visuals Unlimited (tr). **Science Photo Library:** CHARLES D. WINTERS (cra). **76 Dorling Kindersley:** The Natural History Museum, London (tl). **77 Dorling Kindersley:** The Natural History Museum, London (tr). **iStockphoto.com:** Olivier Blondeau (tc). **78 Dorling Kindersley:** The Natural History Museum, London (crb). **Dreamstime.com:** Bogdan Dumitru (tl). **Science Photo Library:** The Natural History Museum, London (tl). **79 Alamy Images:** Siim Sepp (cb). **80 Alamy Images:** Paolo Messina (cr); redsnapper (clb). **Corbis:** James Chororos (tr). **Dreamstime.com:** Joyce Vincent (c). **81 Corbis:** Ritterbach / F1 Online (cb). **Dreamstime.com:** Maurie Hill (c). **83 Dorling Kindersley:** The Natural History Museum, London (ca); The Natural History Museum, London (c). **84-85 Corbis:** Peter Adams / JAI. **86 Alamy Images:** Lightner Collection (tl). **Corbis:** Pascal Deloche / Photononstop (c). **Corbis:** Gator (c / cat). **86-87 Dorling Kindersley:** Maidstone Museum and Bentlift Art Gallery (c). **87 Corbis:** Leemage (tr). **Dorling Kindersley:** The Natural History Museum, London (clb/powder). **Getty Images:** Print Collector (c). **Science Photo Library:** JOEL AREM (cb). **88 Alamy Images:** PjrStudio (cb). **90 Corbis:** Nature Connect (c). **Dorling Kindersley:** The Natural History Museum, London (cb). **Dreamstime.com:** Cjh Photography Llc (cr). **NASA:** JPL / USGS (cb). **Science Photo Library:** DIRK WIERSMA (cl). **91 Alamy Images:** DIRK WIERSMA (tl). **Corbis:** Vittoriano Rastelli (c). **Dreamstime.com:** Daniel Kaesler (cl). **Getty Images:** Sean Gallup (cr). **92-93 Dr.Alexander Van Driessche. 94 Corbis:** Walter Geiersperger (crb). **Dorling Kindersley:** Oxford University Museum of Natural History (ca). **95 Dorling Kindersley:** The Natural History Museum, London (c). **97 Dorling Kindersley:** The Natural History Museum, London (c, cr). **Dreamstime.com:** Mrreporter (tl). **98 Alamy Images:** Shawn Hempel (br). **Corbis:** Mark Schneider / Visuals Unlimited (tl). **Dorling Kindersley:** The Natural History Museum, London (bc). **Dreamstime.com:** Slavapolo (cl). **99 Dorling Kindersley:** The Natural History Museum, London (tl). **Dreamstime.com:** Martina Osmy (cl). **100 Baldi, Home Jewels:** (tl). **Dorling Kindersley:** The Natural History Museum, London (cb, crb). **Dreamstime.com:** Alexxl66 (cb/hammer). **Getty Images:** Siede Preis / Photodisc (ca). **101 Dorling Kindersley:** The Natural History Museum, London (c). **Dreamstime.com:** Inga Nielsen (c). **102 Corbis:** (tc); Visuals Unlimited (crb). **Dorling Kindersley:** The Natural History Museum, London (tl, cla, ftr). **102-103 Dorling Kindersley:** The Natural History Museum, London (c). **103 Alamy Images:** World History Archive (c); John Keeble / VisualGems (cb). **Corbis:** Eric Meola (cr); Mark Schneider / Visuals Unlimited (cla). **Dorling Kindersley:** The Natural History Museum, London (ca). **Dreamstime.com:** Loveliestdreams (tr). **104 Alamy Images:** Melvyn Longhurst China (cb). **Corbis:** AStock (cla); imberly Walker / robertharding (cb). **Dorling Kindersley:** 104The Natural History Museum, London (tr). **105 Corbis:** Huetter, C (c); Asian Art & Archaeology, Inc. (ca). **Dorling Kindersley:** The Natural History Museum, London (tl, tc). **National Museum of Natural History, Smithsonian Institution:** Chip Clark (cb). **Science Photo Library:** DIRK WIERSMA (cl). **106-107 Alamy Images:** Fredrik Stenström. **108 Corbis:** (cl). **Dorling Kindersley:** Christie's Images (clb); The Natural History Museum, London (cra). **Getty Images:** De Agostini / A. Rizzi (cra). **National Museum of Natural History, Smithsonian Institution:** Chip Clark (ca, crb). **Science Photo Library:** DAVID PARKER (cr). **109 Corbis:** PjrStudio (br). **Dreamstime.com:** Ingemar Magnusson (cl). **Getty Images:** Dawid Wapenaar / EyeEm (ca); HECTOR MATA (cra). **National Museum of Natural History, Smithsonian Institution:** Chip Clark (tl, clb). **Science Photo Library:** JOEL AREM (cb). **110 Dorling Kindersley:** The Natural History Museum, London (tl, cb). **Science Photo Library:** ADRIAN DENNIS (tr). **110-111 Alamy Images:** Phil Degginger (c). **111 Alamy Images:** John Cancalosi (cr). **Corbis:** Smithsonian Institution (tr). **Dorling Kindersley:** The Natural History Museum, London (c). **National Museum of Natural History, Smithsonian Institution:** (cb); Chip Clark (ca). **112 Dorling Kindersley:** University of Pennsylvania Museum of Archaeology and Anthropology (cla); The Natural History Museum, London (c). **Dreamstime.com:** Christophe Avril (clb). **113 Dorling Kindersley:** The Natural History Museum, London (cla). **Dreamstime.com:** Ricok (crb). **114 Dorling Kindersley:** The Natural History Museum, London (c). **Dreamstime.com:** Valentyn75 (tr). **114-115 Dorling Kindersley:** The Natural History Museum, London (bc). **115 Alamy Images:** INSADCO Photography (cb); Martin Strmiska (tr). **Dorling Kindersley:** The Natural History Museum, London (tc, cr); The Natural History Museum, London (c). **116 Alamy Images:** Nature Picture Library (c). **Corbis:** ALEXANDER DEMIANCHUK / Reuters (cb). **Dorling Kindersley:** The Natural History Museum, London (cr); The Royal Academy of Music (clb). **Dreamstime.com:** Cristian Mihai Vela (tl). **117 Dorling Kindersley:** Hans-Joachim Schneider (c). **Bridgeman Images:** The Natural History Museum, London (c). **Dorling Kindersley:** The Natural History Museum, London (cr). **Dreamstime.com:** Ra3rn (cb). **118 Dorling Kindersley:** The Natural History Museum, London (cl, tc, c, cb). **119 Dorling Kindersley:** The Natural

History Museum, London (tl, clb, cb, crb). **National Museum of Natural History, Smithsonian Institution:** Chip Clark (tr); Ken Larsen (cla). **120 Corbis:** Walter Geiersperger (l). **Dorling Kindersley:** The Natural History Museum, London (tr); The Natural History Museum, London (c, cb, crb). **Getty Images:** Ron Evans (ca). **120-121 Dreamstime.com:** Phodo1 (c). **121 Alamy Images:** WILDLIFE GmbH (ca). **Dorling Kindersley:** The Natural History Museum, London (tl, tc, tr, c, clb). **Photoshot:** Julie Woodhouse (cra). **122-123 Alamy Images:** lunamarina. **124-125 Alamy Images:** Marvin Dembinsky Photo Associates (c). **126 Dorling Kindersley:** Oxford Museum of Natural History (cb). **127 Dorling Kindersley:** Swedish Museum of Natural History (c); The Natural History Museum, London (c). **128 Alamy Images:** John Cancalosi (c); David Coleman (ca). **Dorling Kindersley:** The Natural History Museum, London (cla, clb, cb). **Dreamstime.com:** Linda Bucklin (tc). **Science Photo Library:** CHRISTIAN DARKIN (clb/shark). **128-129 Fort Hays State University's Sternberg Museum of Natural History:** (t). **129 Dorling Kindersley:** Swedish Museum of Natural History (tr); The Natural History Museum, London (cl). **Dreamstime.com:** Damir Franusic (cr). **130 Alamy Images:** Frans Lanting (clb). **Dorling Kindersley:** Oxford Museum of Natural History (cl); The Natural History Museum, London (tl, cr). **Science Photo Library:** DIRK WIERSMA (tl). **130-131 Dorling Kindersley:** Swedish Museum of Natural History (t). **131 Alamy Images:** Roberto Nistri (cl). **Corbis:** Layne Kennedy (r). **Dorling Kindersley:** The Natural History Museum, London (bl). **Science Photo Library:** MARK A. SCHNEIDER (tl). **132-133 Getty Images:** Witold Skrypczak. **134 Dorling Kindersley:** Geological Museum, University of Copenhagen, Denmark / University Museum of Zoology, Cambridge (cla); Harry Taylor / Trustees of the National Museums Of Scotland (cla/Ichthyostega); The Natural History Museum, London (clb); Institute of Geology and Palaeontology, Tubingen, Germany (crb). **Getty Images:** De Agostini Picture Library (clb/Cynognathus). **Science Photo Library:** LOUISE K. BROMAN (cb). **134-135 Dorling Kindersley:** The Natural History Museum, London (c). **Getty Images:** Wolfgang Kaehler (t). **135 Dorling Kindersley:** The Natural History Museum, London (c). **Dreamstime.com:** Andreas Meyer (tl). **Science Photo Library:** HERVE CONGE, ISM (clb); THE NATURAL HISTORY MUSEUM, LONDON (cl). **136 Corbis:** Ken Lucas (cr). **Getty Images:** DEA / G. CIGOLINI (cl). **137 Alamy Images:** Prisma Archivo (t); Corbin17 (cl). **Dorling Kindersley:** Oxford Museum of Natural History (cr); The Natural History Museum, London (cra); The Sedgwick Museum of Geology. (cb/jaw). **Science Photo Library:** THE NATURAL HISTORY MUSEUM, LONDON (cr). **138 Corbis:** Jonathan Blair (tl). **Dorling Kindersley:** The Senckenberg Nature Museum (tr); The Natural History Museum, London (c). **139 123RF.com:** Michael Rosskothen (cla). **Alamy Images:** Thomas Cockrem (cb). **Corbis:** Ken Lucas (tl). **Dorling Kindersley:** The Natural History Museum, London (tr). **Getty Images:** Eric Van Den Brulle (cr); ANTONIO SCORZA (ca). **SuperStock:** Clive Glen (clb). **140 Dorling Kindersley:** Oxford Museum of Natural History (cla). **Dreamstime.com:** Seanyu (cla). **Science Photo Library:** DIRK WIERSMA (tr). **140-141 Dorling Kindersley:** Senckenberg Gesellschaft Fuer Naturforschugn (c). **141 Dorling Kindersley:** The American Museum of Natural History (crb); The Natural History Museum, London (tl); State Museum of Nature, Stuttgart (cl). **Dreamstime.com:** Seanyu (cra). **142 Alamy Images:** Corbin17 (clb). **Dorling Kindersley:** The Royal Tyrrell Museum of Palaeontology, Alberta, Canada (ca); The Natural History Museum, London (tr); The Senckenberg Gesellschaft Fuer Naturforschugn Museum (cl). **142-143 Dorling Kindersley:** The Natural History Museum, London (c). **143 Dorling Kindersley:** Oxford Museum of Natural History (cla); The Royal Tyrrell Museum of Palaeontology, Alberta, Canada (tc); The Senckenberg Gesellschaft Fuer Naturforschung Museum (crb). **144 Corbis:** Louie Psihoyos (cla); Bernard Weil (c). **Dorling Kindersley:** The Royal Tyrrell Museum of Palaeontology, Alberta, Canada (clb); The Senckenberg Nature Museum, Frankfurt (crb). **145 Alamy Images:** John Cancalosi (tl); WaterFrame (cra); The Natural History Museum, London (cla). **Dorling Kindersley:** Jon Hughes (ftr); The Natural History Museum, London (cr). **Science Photo Library:** MATTEIS (cla). **146-147 Getty Images:** Spencer Platt (c). **148 Alamy Images:** Encyclopaedia Britannica / Universal Images Group Limited (cb); Amy Toensing / National Geographic Image Collection (c). **Dorling Kindersley:** The Natural History Museum, London (tr, cr). **Science Photo Library:** JAIME CHIRINOS (cla). **149 Alamy Images:** Pat Canova (crb); WaterFrame_sta (clb). **Dorling Kindersley:** The Natural History Museum, London (cra). **Science Photo Library:** UCL, GRANT MUSEUM OF ZOOLOGY (t); The Natural History Museum, London (fcla, cr). **Roman Uchytel:** Roman Uchytel (crb/Hyracotherium). **150 Dorling Kindersley:** The Natural History Museum, London (cla); National Museum of Wales (clb); The Natural History Museum, London (cb); The Oxford Museum of Natural History (crb). **150-151 Dorling Kindersley:** The Natural History Museum, London (ca, cb). **151 Alamy Images:** The Natural History Museum, London (tc). **Dorling Kindersley:** The Natural History Museum, London (tc, cr). **Science Photo Library:** The Natural History Museum, London (tc). **152-153 Photoshot:** World Pictures. **154-155 Alamy Images:** Frans Lanting. **156-157 Dreamstime.com:** Milanmarkovic. **157 naturepl.com:** Wild Wonders of Europe / Lundgren (br); Nature Production (cla). **162-163 naturepl.com:** Alex Mustard. **164 Science Photo Library:** GILLES MERMET (ca). **165 Science Photo Library:** GILLES MERMET (crb). **Science Photo Library:** GILLES MERMET (crb). **172-173 naturepl.com:** GEORGETTE DOUWMA. **176-177 Photoshot:** Imagebroker. **181 Dorling Kindersley:** The Natural History Museum, London (cr). **182-183 Getty Images:** Ullstein bild. **184 Alamy Images:** Scott Camazine. **185 Corbis:** Walter Geiersperger (br). **186 Dorling Kindersley:** Oxford University Museum of Natural History (crb); The Oxford University Museum of Natural History (c); The Natural History Museum, London (cl, tr, cr, clb, cb)

All other images © Dorling Kindersley

For further information see:
www.dkimages.com